The
NOURISHING
COOK

Leah Itsines

♥

The NOURISHING COOK

Pan Macmillan Australia

CONTENTS

Hi guys!

Thank you so much for joining me on this health journey. My name is Leah Itsines and I'm a food blogger and self-taught cook. I'm on a mission to help people make healthy eating an easy lifestyle choice by building CREATIVITY and CONFIDENCE in the kitchen.

This isn't your ordinary cookbook; it's a creative guide that will inspire you to have a go and learn for yourself just how simple it is to cook delicious and nutritious meals that everyone will want to eat. It is designed to help you add more SPICE and LOVE to your diet and is full of recipes that will leave you looking and feeling absolutely amazing. I created this book to share my philosophy that BALANCE is the key ingredient when it comes to leading a wholesome life. If you enjoy a varied diet that is flexible and full of wholefoods, you needn't deprive yourself of anything!

In Part 1 of *The Nourishing Cook*, I explain why I cook the way I do by exploring the science behind nutrition and balance. I show you the basics of cooking and prepping your kitchen so you can build a perfect, nourishing meal, which includes my favourite tips and staples to kickstart your own creative journey. Part 2 illustrates what my typical day on a plate looks like and how it can be easily altered to suit your daily requirements. Lastly, Part 3 is a collection of my simple and super tasty recipes that are so close to my heart. All the recipes are bursting with flavour and jam-packed with the best fresh produce.

Raised in a Greek household, I grew up surrounded by the love of food. The celebrations, the family gatherings . . . everything revolved around FOOD and FAMILY. As I grow older, cooking for myself and my family has become super important to me as it takes me back to that happy place where I feel truly at home. I learnt everything I know from my grandmothers and mother. When I was in primary school, Mum would pick me up from school and drive me straight to the supermarket to buy groceries for that night's dinner. I absolutely LOVED this as Mum would let me choose all the ingredients and even let me 'pay' with her credit card (oh, how I wish that still happened! Ha ha!).

People often ask me how I taught myself to cook, and all I can say is that I learnt by DOING. I took the knowledge that my family passed down to me and created my own classics, from simple breakfasts like pancakes and yummy frittatas, to delicious mains like fresh homemade pasta and pizza. The process of cooking, for me, is very therapeutic. When you cook for yourself, you can control all the ingredients you use. This helps you nourish your body with all the good stuff – leaving out all the nasties! So if you're new to cooking, don't be scared. Just get in the kitchen and it will only be a matter of time before you surprise yourself with some amazing skills and healthy results.

I want nothing more than to share this book with you and I hope it inspires you to cook more and thoroughly enjoy the nourishing food you eat. Let this book help you find the balance that suits your lifestyle and discover a HAPPIER and HEALTHIER YOU.

Leah xx

CREATIVE COOKING for NUTRITIOUS MEALS

Here is all the information you need to inspire CREATIVITY and CONFIDENCE in the kitchen. Learn about:

♥ The importance of nutrition (see page 12).

♥ Macronutrients and why they are crucial to good health (see page 14).

♥ How to build a nourishing plate (see page 18).

♥ My secret tools and tips for setting up your kitchen (see pages 20–29).

♥ How to make veggies, eggs, chicken and beef extra tasty with my cooking basics (see pages 30–41).

- WHY IS -
NUTRITION IMPORTANT?

Creating nutritious meals is all about understanding the basics so you can make healthier choices.

We all need food and water to survive. But how do our bodies work when we feed ourselves? A BALANCED diet allows our bodies to function properly, remain healthy and grow. When we eat, our bodies break down the nutrients of the meal. These nutrients can be divided into macronutrients and micronutrients. Macronutrients are energy-providing nutrients that our bodies need in large amounts – protein, carbohydrates and fats. Micronutrients, like vitamins and minerals, are needed in small amounts but are also crucial.

Nutrient-dense foods provide the building blocks that allow our bodies to maintain muscle mass, fuel our brains and organs, and grow, repair and build our muscle faster. Every person has different nutritional requirements and needs. For example, if you're super active, you need to ensure you are consuming enough energy and protein. This is because protein is broken down into amino acids which are then used by the body to build and repair muscle tissue after working out. So eating the right combination of food can help your body recover at a faster rate.

Not only is our food intake vital for good health but so is our WATER INTAKE. As our bodies can't store water, we need to replenish our bodies every day. For women, we should be aiming to drink two litres of water a day.

Think of your body like a car: it needs fuel, oil and air-filled tyres to run efficiently. This is identical to your body, which needs nutrient-dense food, water, rest, sleep and sunlight to be able to perform at an optimum level. This is why it is important to fuel our bodies correctly. It's not about *how much* we eat, but *what* we eat, that helps our bodies run smoothly. By understanding the health benefits of everything you consume then putting this into practice, you are taking the right steps towards a HEALTHIER, HAPPIER lifestyle and, of course, living life to the FULLEST.

Need a mood boost?

Low levels of vitamin D can put you at risk of depression and anxiety. Luckily, the sun is not the only source of vitamin D! Eating 100 g of mushrooms left in the sun for an hour (even in winter) will provide you with a large amount of your vitamin D requirements.

Need a tummy helper?

Eat more foods that are pickled or fermented, such as sauerkraut and pickles, to boost your intake of live cultures, which are great for gut health!

Need more iron?

Iron found in animal products like red meat is absorbed much more easily than plant-based sources like spinach. To supercharge your iron absorption (and help prevent a foggy brain, and low energy and immunity), eat it with brightly coloured orange fruit and veggies, which contain vitamin C. Also, try not to drink alcohol or caffeine when eating iron-rich foods as these can prevent iron absorption as well.

- WHAT ARE -
MACRONUTRIENTS?

Macronutrients are specific nutrients that your body needs in large quantities. There are three kinds of 'macros': carbohydrates, protein and fats. All of these provide you with the ESSENTIAL energy that you need to fuel your body and are the components for creating a nutritious meal. So how do macronutrients work in your body? And what happens if you're lacking in one or another? Your body simply can't function to its full potential without a BALANCED amount. With the help of Lyndi Cohen, The Nude Nutritionist, I've explained how each macro affects your body and outlined my favourite sources of protein, carbs and fats.

Tip: Eat black beans and rice together to help you get all your essential amino acids, which are the building blocks of protein. Other great vegan combos include peanut butter and toast, and black beans in a tortilla.

PROTEIN

When it comes to fuelling your body, protein plays a crucial role. It helps build and repair muscle, ensures your organs function properly, strengthens your hair and nails and promotes clear skin. Restricting protein-rich foods will cause your body to slow down and this can have a massive impact on your energy levels and physical strength. Other signs that you may not be getting enough protein include body aches, difficulty losing weight and low immunity. Speak to your GP if you are experiencing any of these symptoms.

RED MEAT

Red meat, such as beef, lamb or pork, is one of the best sources of animal protein. 100 g of meat contains roughly 30 g of protein. It also contains loads of micro-nutrients, such as iron and zinc, making it an all-round winner. Zinc is valuable to your body as it promotes immunity, growth and healthy development. Iron is also super important as it carries oxygen around your body and keeps your cells, skin, hair and nails in top condition. Red meat can be cooked in many ways and comes in various cuts like steak, chops, cutlets or mince. I'm not a huge steak eater, but I love a lean eye fillet as it's lovely and tender when grilled.

BLACK BEANS

These wholesome beans boast an impressive 21 g of protein per 100 g! Not as far behind red meat as people would think. Black beans are also loaded with fibre and great for gut health. My favourite way to cook black beans is in Baked Eggs with Black Beans (see page 83).

TOFU

Tofu, a popular vegan option, is made by curdling fresh soy milk, pressing it into a solid block then cooling it. This process is similar to traditional cheese-making. It can be cooked in MANY different ways, such as grilling, pan-frying and even scrambling (see my recipe on page 79), to suit your desired texture: smooth, soft, crispy or crunchy. There are three types of tofu – soft, firm and extra-firm – so be aware of these when you're at the supermarket. Tofu is a great source of plant-based protein, giving you 10 g of protein per 125 g.

EGGS

Eggs are an ideal protein source for both before and after your workout. They are easy to prepare, contain plenty of vitamins and healthy fats, and will keep you feeling full. One egg will give you an impressive 6 g of protein! I ALWAYS buy free-range: this means that the hens are allowed to roam free instead of being cooped up in a cage. Look for the lowest number of hens per hectare on the box – 1500 hens at an absolute maximum. The fewer hens per hectare, the more room they have to run around.

CHICKEN

Chicken contains around 30 g of protein per 100 g, making it a wonderful protein-packed addition to any lunch or dinner. It cooks quickly and is extremely versatile. I've shared my cooking basics for chicken on page 38, but another easy way to cook it is to coat the chicken in a dry rub then grill it. Drizzle the grilled chicken with a touch of extra-virgin olive oil and a squeeze of lemon, to keep it super juicy! Remember to look out for certified free-range chickens, as you would eggs.

Tip: Tofu can be super watery and no oil-based marinade will stick to it without a little DIY water extraction! To do this, cut the tofu into the size you need. Place it on two sheets of paper towel and place two more sheets on top. Place something heavy on the paper towel and leave for 10 minutes to draw out the water. Then you're ready to marinate!

CARBOHYDRATES

One of the biggest nutritional misconceptions is that carbohydrates are bad for you! Your body needs carbs for energy – the key is to choose the HEALTHIER, slow-burning complex carbs, instead of avoiding them all together. To give you a quick run-down, carbohydrates are divided into two groups: simple carbs and complex carbs. Simple carbs are fast-burning and include foods such as doughnuts, table sugar, syrups and sugary cereals. These foods will give you a sharp spike in energy levels but the boost won't last long. Once the energy wears off, your blood-sugar levels will drop quickly and you'll be left feeling tired and searching for your next energy hit. Complex carbs are typically less refined and will give you longer, more sustained energy. These include a variety of fruit, vegetables and grains. I've listed some of my favourites below.

SWEET POTATO

Sweet potato tastes exactly how it sounds! It's a SWEET-tasting potato that's loaded with vitamin C, which can boost immunity and help keep your skin clear . . . what's not to love? Sweet potato is a fantastic substitute for white potato as they have a very similar texture. For added fibre, always cook sweet potato with the skin on.

BROWN RICE

Compared to white rice, brown rice contains more nutrients and is less processed, which is good news for your health! White rice starts off as brown rice but is then processed, stripping the grain of some of its beneficial micronutrients like iron, vitamins, zinc and magnesium. Brown rice is not put through this process so it retains those nutrients. Other great wholegrains to try include freekeh, amaranth and barley.

OATS

Oats are one of my favourite carbs! They are super versatile and a great way to start your morning as they will keep you full for longer. They can help lower cholesterol levels and are packed full of the vitamins and minerals that our bodies need. Oats can be used as a base for almost any breakfast smoothie.

QUINOA

Quinoa (pronounced keenwah) has reached 'superfood' status over the past few years AND it's naturally gluten-free. Quinoa also contains a good amount of plant-based protein and fibre so it's a great wholegrain to help you ramp up your intake and keep you feeling fuller for longer.

Tip: Rice is naturally gluten-free. If you're coeliac, check the label before buying to be certain there is no contamination.

FATS

Fat can be a frightening word, but it's so misunderstood. Over the years, we have been inundated with opinions on how 'bad' fat supposedly is for our bodies, but this isn't the case! Fat has many important functions, including stabilising MOOD and ENERGY levels. But not all fats are created equal. Saturated fats and trans fats – like those commonly found in deep-fried fast food and packaged or processed foods – aren't great for heart health and should only be eaten in moderation. The fats we want in our diet are unsaturated fats – like polyunsaturated or monounsaturated fats – conveniently found in plant-based foods and fish.

NUTS AND SEEDS

Nuts are a great source of healthy fat, which can help boost your heart health, keep you feeling fuller for longer and assist in regulating your hormones. Aim for a handful of almonds, cashews, walnuts, macadamias or pistachios a day. Seeds – such as pumpkin seeds, sunflower seeds, flaxseeds and chia seeds – contain plenty of fibre and plant-based protein. Nuts and seeds are great to snack on or add them to breakfast bowls, smoothies or salads.

OILS

Oils like extra-virgin olive oil, sesame oil, sunflower oil and peanut oil are perfect for adding healthy fats to your diet. In fact, using oil in your salad dressing will help your body absorb fat-soluble nutrients, like vitamins A, D, E and K.

AVOCADO

Rest assured – when you Instagram your smashed avo, there's science to back up your healthy choice! Avocado is virtually the only 'fruit' that contains monounsaturated fat and it is free from cholesterol and sodium, which are added bonuses. Working ¼ avocado into your day will give you a great source of healthy fat, while leaving room for other nourishing foods. After all – variety is the key to a healthy diet!

FISH

Fish contains plenty of omega-3 and healthy fats. Salmon, tuna, sardines and mackerel are all oily-based fish that are perfect for getting those good fats into your day. Studies have shown that eating oily-based fish as a part of your diet can help lower your triglycerides by 25 per cent. Triglycerides are a type of fat in your bloodstream, so reducing them is great for your overall health.

Tip: Be sure to close the lid of your extra-virgin olive oil tightly to prevent it oxidising and losing antioxidants. It's worth investing in a high-quality cold-pressed extra-virgin olive oil, as regular olive oil doesn't have as many antioxidants and phytonutrients to help nourish your body.

- THE PERFECT -
NOURISHING PLATE

Now that you understand the importance of consuming nutrient-dense foods for good health, let's put it into practice. Here's what a healthy, balanced plate should look like. If you use these proportions as a guide in all your cooking it will give you the base to experiment with different foods!

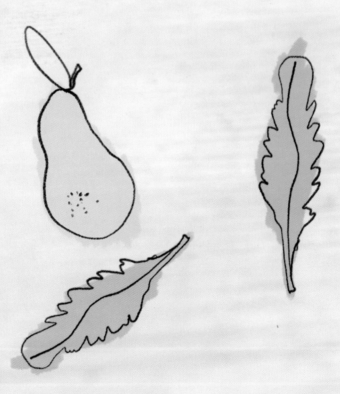

FOR BALANCE

50% Veggies
and Salads

25% Complex Carbs
See page 16 for
options.

25% Protein
Cooked in a healthy fat like
olive oil. See page 15 for
protein options.

AND GOOD HEALTH

– WHAT TO KNOW –
BEFORE YOU SHOP

Many people find food shopping super boring, but luckily I'm one of those crazy people who looks forward to it! I love being able to walk the aisles and find new and exciting fruits and veggies that give me inspiration to create FUN and FLAVOURSOME meals. But I know it can be difficult for some, so I have compiled a list of my top tips to think about before you head to the supermarket. This will help you to be mindful about what you're purchasing and why, and make informed decisions about how to build a nourishing plate every day of the week.
I hope that by learning these preparation basics, you will then be able to adapt the rules to suit your own life and come up with your own INCREDIBLE creations!

PRE-PLAN MEALS

Pre-planning doesn't mean 'meal prepping'. It means PLAN your meals. I like to know what I'm having for every meal so I'm able to whip it up without wasting any time! Listing your meals for the week is an easy way to stay on track. Writing a shopping list is also useful so you know exactly what you need, how much you need and when you'll need it for! I usually shop on Sunday for Monday, Tuesday and Wednesday and shop on Wednesday for the rest of the week. This allows me to buy fresh veggies and meats without wastage.

BUY IN BULK

Bulk-buying will save you time and money and it's a great way to feed large families. If you find meat on special buy in bulk, then portion and freeze. Some veggies freeze really well too – see page 24 for a guide. Bulk-buying canned goods with a long shelf-life, like tomatoes, vegetables and tuna, is a fantastic way to make sure you always have healthy food in the cupboard. Oats, grains and spices are also cheaper when bought in bulk and you'll never be stuck for inspiration! See page 23 for my pantry staples.

GET EVERYONE INVOLVED

If your partner is in it with you, you'll have a much easier time sticking to your goals and smashing it in the kitchen. Have a chat to the people you live with and let them know that eating healthily and changing your lifestyle is super important to you, and hopefully they'll get on board too!

TRY NEW FOODS

Broaden your horizons by eating a variety of food. Try new veggies, taste new flavours, add new ingredients. Have a look through my recipes and find a specific vegetable, flavour or cuisine you have never tried before and give it a go. For example, the stigma around vegan or vegetarian meals is that they are bland, boring and leafy . . . but not mine! Try to have a meat-free Monday this week by picking one recipe from The Veggie Patch chapter on page 197.

BE INFORMED

Knowing where your food comes from and exactly what it contains is vital for a healthy lifestyle. This is usually overlooked by most people because the information is not readily accessible unless you do your own research. We are becoming increasingly passionate about our land, animal welfare and sustainability. And rightly so. We all talk about putting the right things into our bodies, nourishing ourselves with the good stuff . . . but we also need to ask ourselves where this food comes from, which is equally as important – for our health and our environment.

PACKAGED AND PROCESSED

A lot of big corporations fill foods with excess salt, sugar and additives because they're cheap and make products more appealing. By doing this to benefit their company, these excess ingredients go straight into your body giving you NO benefit whatsoever! Make sure you're looking at your labels to ensure there are no additives such as MSG, artificial sweeteners, BHA and BHT (these are found in gum, potato chips and cereals), artificial food dyes or excessive amounts of salt or sugar.

OUT-OF-SEASON CROPS

Ever seen a fruit at your local grocer and think, *'They're here already?!'* If the food is not in season locally, it is sometimes shipped from other parts of the world, which can dramatically affect the taste and is damaging to the environment. The distance it takes for the food to be transported to you is measured in 'food miles'. The longer the distance, the more greenhouse gases are released into the atmosphere and the bigger the impact on the environment. That's why it is important to look for local products and ensure that the product is in season. For example, mangoes are not a year-round fruit. They are in their prime from September to March, so if you see some in May, June or July . . . you know they were probably imported from elsewhere!

CLOSE THE KNOWLEDGE GAP

When I was a child (hilarious story . . . don't judge!), I honestly believed that sausages grew out of the ground and vegetables were made at the shops. I know, ridiculous, right? As I grew up I started to learn more about where food came from and what happened to get it from farm to plate. I believe we should teach ourselves and our children this process so that we truly understand and appreciate our food, farmers and environment. Educating children about health and nutrition should be a major priority as this is the most influential time of our lives. Teaching, inspiring and implementing healthy eating habits will help children to make balanced and informed lifestyle choices as they develop into adults.

- MY MUST-HAVE -
KITCHEN STAPLES

If you know me, you'll know that my pantry, fridge and freezer are always PACKED with food. My staples make up the foundation of my kitchen and I couldn't cook without them. If you have an ABUNDANCE of these items, you'll never be stuck for ideas!

FRIDGE

- **FRESH VEGGIES:** I LOVE fresh veggies – they are so versatile and can be used in every meal so they'll never go to waste. Veggies such as beetroot, broccoli, carrots and cauliflower are easy to cook and have a long shelf-life.

- **EGGS:** Eggs are a staple for most of my breakfasts and a key ingredient for baking. I ALWAYS run out of eggs when I need them so remember to keep your fridge well stocked to avoid an emergency run to the supermarket!

- **GREEK YOGHURT:** Yoghurt is the best. I have it in the morning with some muesli or after dinner with some honey and berries. Natural Greek yoghurt contains protein and promotes overall digestion.

- **BIG BOTTLED WATER:** WATER, WATER, WATER! I always fill up my fridge with big reusable bottles of water – this makes it super easy to grab and go. It also encourages me to drink more and stay hydrated. Try to invest in reusable bottles to cut down on plastic waste.

- **FRESH HERBS:** Fresh herbs go in EVERYTHING. They simply make every dish more flavoursome and take you from amateur cook to MasterChef! Fresh herbs don't last long in the fridge, which is why many people would rather buy them dried. I buy one packet of fresh herbs at a time and use as much as I can (experiment, experiment, experiment!) so there is no wastage. They may not last long in the fridge, but they do in the garden. Plant some parsley, coriander, basil and mint and you'll not only be a MasterChef, but a pro-gardener too!

PANTRY

- **SPICES:** Say NO to bland foods! Spices and seasonings make your meals sing with flavour. My favourites are salt, pepper, chilli, garlic and coriander (see more on page 28).

- **OATS:** Oats make delicious porridge, muesli, bliss balls, smoothies and so much more! They provide long-lasting energy and are perfect for breakfast or a snack.

- **PASTA:** Pasta is quick, easy and yummy. Stock your pantry with spaghetti, penne and spirals for the perfect variety of pasta. I often opt for wholemeal pasta as it keeps me fuller for longer.

- **RICE:** I always buy brown rice or basmati rice in 10 kg bulk bags. They have a really long shelf-life and are super cheap!

- **CANNED GOODS:** Canned veggies and legumes are essential. Crushed tomatoes are useful to help whip up a pasta sauce, and a four-bean mix is an incredible addition to any salad! Keep canned corn and black beans on hand for a mid-week Mexican night, and also chickpeas – you never know when you'll need some hummus!

FREEZER

There are MANY foods that are fine to buy in bulk and freeze, but there are also some that don't freeze so well. It is essential to know what you can freeze and how long you can store it in the freezer before it spoils.

WHAT CAN I FREEZE?

- **SOUPS:** Make soup in bulk and freeze. That way, if you're home late and rushing for dinner, you can just defrost and eat!

- **FRUIT AND VEGETABLES:** You can buy some staples already frozen such as corn, peas, berries and other fruit. Veggies such as spinach and kale, which usually have a short shelf-life, can be blanched and frozen. Slice or chop tomato, zucchini or onion and store it in a tight zip-lock bag in the freezer. When you want to use them, defrost the veggies in the fridge overnight then use them for a quick stir fry, sauce or side dish. Veggies can last in the freezer for up to 3 months.

- **PASTA SAUCE:** Don't throw out leftover sauce – FREEZE IT! It comes in handy when you feel like pasta but don't have the time or energy to make the sauce from scratch. Keep in the freezer for up to 3 months.

- **BREAD:** If you're the only one who eats bread in your house, try popping the loaf in the freezer and taking a slice as you need it. It's a great way to avoid waste and it will stay fresh. Bread will freeze for up to 1 month.

- **MEAT, FISH AND CHICKEN:** Freeze meat and fish in meal-size portions so it's easy to defrost when you need it. Uncooked meat, fish and chicken can keep in the freezer for 3–6 months.

- **GRATED CHEESE:** Have you ever bought a huge packet of grated cheese and had lots left over? Don't let it go to waste! Cheese is GREAT in the freezer – because it melts the same as before it was frozen. It will keep in the freezer for up to 4 months.

- **FRESH HERBS:** Fill an ice-cube tray with chopped fresh herbs then pour some olive oil into each hole and freeze. This saves on waste and you can just add a cube when you are cooking a stir-fry or pasta sauce. These are best used within 1 month.

WHAT CAN'T I FREEZE?

- **RAW EGGS IN THE SHELL:** The liquid inside will expand, crack the shell and make them unusable.

- **VEGETABLES WITH A HIGH WATER CONTENT:** Veggies such as lettuce and cucumber become waterlogged once thawed, turning them nasty.

- **MILK/YOGHURT:** When a dairy product like milk or yoghurt is thawed, it can become super lumpy!

HOW TO THAW FOOD

Let's not talk about room temperature . . . PLEASE! Thawing out food at room temperature leaves the door wide open for bacterial growth. There's a 'danger zone' for bacteria growth in foods, and that is between 5–60°C. Room temperature sits somewhere between 20–22°C. So leaving your food for any length of time in that danger zone can cause some serious problems. Instead, the safest way is to pop the frozen food in the fridge to thaw overnight. Alternatively, if you are short on time, you can defrost it in the microwave – but make sure you use the defrost setting as you don't want to cook the meat!

MY FAVOURITE
FRUITS

WATERMELON

Watermelon tastes delicious in fresh juice.
It's over 90 per cent water and is rich in
electrolytes so it's perfect for hydration!
My favourite summer blend is watermelon,
lime, mint and coconut water. Coconut
water has been named nature's 'Gatorade'
and it's also high in electrolytes, so this
blend is what your body needs when
you've been in the summer sun!

BLUEBERRIES

Berries are full of antioxidants
so they're a great addition to yoghurt
in the morning, smoothies for snacks
or to top ice-cream for dessert!

ORANGES

There is nothing better than a fresh OJ. It's packed with vitamin C, and you KNOW you'll feel amazing afterwards. Always try to squeeze your own and steer clear of pre-packaged juices with added sugars.

NEED TO RIPEN FRUIT? This is a SUPER easy trick; all you need is the unripened fruit, a banana and a paper bag! Throw the unripened fruit into the bag with the banana and leave for a day. Bananas release a lot of ethylene, which helps ripen fruit nearby.

SAVE MY BANANAS: Wrap the top of your banana with plastic wrap and they can last an extra five days without going brown!

LEMONS

Freshly squeezed lemon juice is delicious in salad dressings! A squeeze of lemon juice can also save fruit that goes brown easily (like apples, avocado, pears, bananas and peaches). If you're only using half the fruit, squeeze some lemon juice over it before putting it in the fridge.

PINEAPPLE

Fun fact: pineapple contains an enzyme called bromelain, which breaks down proteins and basically attacks your mouth! But as soon as you swallow, your saliva and stomach acid take over and save you. Cool thing is you can eliminate the enzyme by grilling or heating the pineapple. Pineapple is also high in vitamin C, which keeps our immunity strong. So pineapple paired with oranges will leave you feeling on top of the world!

GARLIC

I owe my love of garlic to my yiayia who uses a hundred cloves of garlic in all her cooking! There are so many ways to enjoy garlic. Try it in dips, spreads, pasta sauces, salads, baking . . . the list is endless!

SALT

Salt is my number-one staple because it makes dishes so much tastier. My family calls me the salt queen because I always add a little bit more! Top quality salt is good for us in moderation. It is essential for the body as it can sustain hydration levels and maintain our electrolyte balance for smooth functioning organs.

PEPPER

Pepper is joined at the hip with salt. If a dish has salt, it needs a little pepper to balance out the flavour!

CORIANDER

Coriander has a beautiful taste and it goes with LOTS of different foods! My favourite way to use it is to pair it with mint and throw it in a salad.

CHILLI

A lot of people don't like chilli because it's too hot . . . but a LITTLE bit of chilli can boost the flavour of a meal, times ten! If you're not usually a chilli-lover, try adding just a small amount to your next meal and you'll notice a delicious difference.

MY FAVOURITE

HERBS & SPICES

- COOKING BASICS -
VEGGIES

This table will become your new best friend. When you're not cooking my delicious recipes, keep these pages open in your kitchen for your day-to-day cooking advice. It is a super useful tool if you are starting out on your healthy journey and aren't sure how to SPICE UP your diet with new vegetables. Many veggies are confusing and some are awful raw (eggplant, I'm looking at you!) but all are INCREDIBLE when cooked properly. Learning the basics of cooking, tasting, testing and eating can inspire your inner chef. This information will help you understand cooking times and temperatures, identify when a veggie is cooked and which style of cooking is best (and worst!) for each vegetable.

VEGETABLE	ROAST	STEAM
ARTICHOKE	**Time:** 1 hour and 10 minutes **Temperature:** 200°C **Notes:** Artichoke is a funny one! Always chop off the top point, around ¼ of the way down. Place stem-side down on a baking tray then drizzle over some olive oil and a pinch of salt. It's cooked when completely soft and lightly golden brown. **Pair with:** Salmon and salad.	**Time:** 25–30 minutes **Notes:** Always chop off the top point, around ¼ of the way down. A steamed artichoke is cooked when you can easily insert a knife through the middle. **Pair with:** A squeeze of lemon and salt and pepper will do the trick.
ASPARAGUS	**Time:** 12–15 minutes **Temperature:** 180°C **Notes:** Always trim the woody end of the stem as it can be hard and unappealing. The thinner the asparagus, the more tender when cooked. It's cooked when soft and lightly golden brown. **Pair with:** Steak and mash.	**Time:** 7–10 minutes **Notes:** Always trim the woody end of the stem as it can be hard and unappealing. Steamed asparagus is cooked when it's tender, but be careful not to over-cook! **Pair with:** Breakfast! Toast and smashed avocado.

VEGETABLE	ROAST	STEAM
BEETROOT	**Time:** 30–40 minutes **Temperature:** 180°C **Notes:** Beets are fabulous in the oven. Try not to roast them whole as this will take ages. Opt for thin slices or small wedges. Ensure they are fully cooked by poking a fork into the middle. If it slides through with ease, they're ready! **Pair with:** Roasted sweet potato to bulk up any salad!	**Time:** 30 minutes **Notes:** Cut the beetroot into small wedges so it cooks evenly. Ensure they're fully cooked by poking a fork into the middle. If it slides through with ease, they're ready! **Pair with:** A squeeze of lemon, always. Such a great combo!
BOK CHOY	**Time:** 5–10 minutes **Temperature:** 180°C **Notes:** Bok choy is a super watery vegetable so it doesn't need to roast for long as it will wilt too much. Cut in half lengthways before roasting. **Pair with:** A splash of soy sauce!	**Time:** 4–6 minutes **Notes:** Bok choy can hold lots of water so don't over-cook. It may become waterlogged if left in the steamer. Cut in half lengthways before steaming. **Pair with:** Chilli, sesame seeds and a splash of soy sauce.
BROCCOLI	**Time:** 25–30 minutes **Temperature:** 180°C **Notes:** Cut into florets. Broccoli can burn easily, so always keep an eye on it. Poke a fork in the floret to make sure they're cooked; if soft (and lightly browned), they're ready! **Pair with:** Hummus. It's incredible!	**Time:** 3–5 minutes **Notes:** It's very easy to over-cook broccoli. You want it tender with a little crunch. I recommend cutting into big florets so they steam evenly over 5 minutes. **Pair with:** A pinch of salt and a squeeze of lemon.
BRUSSELS SPROUTS	**Time:** 25–30 minutes **Temperature:** 180°C **Notes:** Cut the sprouts in half and coat in olive oil and a pinch of salt to make them extra tasty. If you like them a little more golden, leave in the oven a little while longer. **Pair with:** Parmesan cheese! This is a hugely underrated combination!	**Time:** 3–5 minutes **Notes:** You always want a little crunch to your sprouts. So taste-test halfway through as they're easy to over-cook and then become mushy. Leave them whole to steam. **Pair with:** Olive oil, a squeeze of lemon, and salt and pepper! A much-loved staple in my household.
CABBAGE	**Time:** 20–25 minutes **Temperature:** 180°C **Notes:** Cut into 4 cm thick wedges and lay flat on baking paper. Coat in olive oil, salt and pepper. **Pair with:** A steak, carrots and mashed potato.	**Time:** 10 minutes **Notes:** Cut into 4 cm thick wedges and place in the steamer. Taste-test a little while through as they're easy to over-cook and then become mushy. **Pair with:** Salted butter and a little pepper.

VEGETABLE	ROAST	STEAM
CAPSICUM	**Time:** 20–30 minutes **Temperature:** 180°C **Notes:** Cut into 3 cm thick strips and add olive oil and salt and pepper to bring out the flavour. The capsicum is done when they're super soft. **Pair with:** My amazing Roasted capsicum and semi-dried tomato dip on page 129.	**Time:** 2–4 minutes **Notes:** Cut into 3 cm thick strips and keep your eye on them as they will steam quickly. **Pair with:** Olive oil and garlic. Yum!
CARROT	**Time:** 25–35 minutes **Temperature:** 180°C **Notes:** Roast whole carrots until soft on the inside and crunchy and golden brown on the outside. **Pair with:** Chicken and salad.	**Time:** 5–7 minutes **Notes:** Carrots can be steamed whole. Don't over-cook as they can become mushy. You want it tender with a little crunch. **Pair with:** Any protein!
CAULIFLOWER	**Time:** 25–35 minutes **Temperature:** 180°C **Notes:** Cut into florets. Poke a fork in the floret to make sure they're cooked; if soft (and lightly browned), they're ready! **Pair with:** Broccoli, carrot and mashed potato.	**Time:** 5–8 minutes **Notes:** Cut into florets. Don't over-cook as they can become mushy. You want it tender with a little crunch. **Pair with:** A pizza! These steamed florets will go a lovely golden brown after a little while in the oven.
CORN	**Time:** 30–35 minutes **Temperature:** 180°C **Notes:** Roast corn on the cob. Turn the corn after 15 minutes so they roast evenly. **Pair with:** An amazing salted butter!	**Time:** 10–15 minutes **Notes:** Yellow and white corn have a very similar taste, so don't be scared if you have white kernels! Corn can be steamed on the cob and off the cob. **Pair with:** Chopped avocado, tomato, coriander and salt and pepper to make a yummy salsa!
EGGPLANT	**Time:** 20–25 minutes **Temperature:** 180°C **Notes:** Slice the eggplant lengthways or crossways 1 cm thick. Then sprinkle with salt and squeeze out the excess water to remove the bitterness. **Pair with:** Assorted roasted veggies (like capsicum, beetroot, pumpkin and zucchini) in a wrap.	**AVOID**
GREEN BEANS	**Time:** 10–15 minutes **Temperature:** 180°C **Notes:** Cut the tips and tails off the beans before placing them in the oven. Once roasted, they'll go super soft and golden brown. **Pair with:** A pinch of salt, garlic and a squeeze of lemon.	**Time:** 5 minutes **Notes:** Cut the tips and tails off the beans before placing them in the steamer. Be careful not to over-cook as beans can lose their flavour! **Pair with:** My Coconut and chilli bean salad on page 116.

VEGETABLE	ROAST	STEAM
KALE	**Time:** 15–20 minutes **Temperature:** 180°C **Notes:** Remove central stem and rip leaves into pieces the size of your palm. Add a sprinkle of salt and some chilli flakes for a hit of flavour. The kale is done when semi-wilted or they becomes crunchy like chips! **Pair with:** Brekky! It's amazing with eggs on toast.	**Time:** 5 minutes **Notes:** Remove central stem and rip leaves into pieces the size of your palm. Kale wilts quickly, so don't let it over-cook! **Pair with:** Use kale as a colourful base on your plate, and top with steak and mash.
BOK CHOY	**Time:** 5–10 minutes **Temperature:** 180°C **Notes:** Bok choy is a super watery vegetable so don't roast them for long as they'll wilt too much. Cut in half lengthways before roasting. **Pair with:** A splash of soy sauce!	**Time:** 4–6 minutes **Notes:** Bok choy can hold lots of water so don't over-cook. They may become waterlogged if left in the steamer. Cut in half lengthways before steaming. **Pair with:** Chilli, sesame seeds and a splash of soy sauce.
MUSHROOMS	**Time:** 15–20 minutes **Temperature:** 180°C **Notes:** Mushrooms are technically a fungus but for the purpose of this table, I'm going to say they're my favourite vegetable! Place seasoning underneath the mushrooms so it soaks in. They're ready when they're soft and get a nice colour on top. **Pair with:** Olive oil, chilli, garlic, parsley, salt and pepper – delicious!	AVOID
ONION	**Time:** 10 minutes **Temperature:** 180°C **Notes:** Cut the onion into rings and sprinkle with salt before roasting – this brings out the flavour! **Pair with:** A burger! Bun, patty, lettuce, tomato and you're good to go!	AVOID
POTATO	**Time:** 45–50 minutes **Temperature:** 180°C **Notes:** Cut in half for a delicious roast potato! If you're short on time, steam them for 5–6 minutes beforehand. Poke a fork into the middle and if soft, they're ready! **Pair with:** Olive oil, vinegar, dried oregano, salt and pepper. Best combo!	**Time:** 30 minutes **Notes:** Cut in half and steam until the potato is super soft and light. Poke a fork through the middle and if it slides through with ease, they're ready! **Pair with:** Butter, chives, garlic, salt and pepper to make the perfect mashed potato.

VEGETABLE	ROAST	STEAM
PUMPKIN	**Time:** 30–40 minutes **Temperature:** 180°C **Notes:** Use a sharp knife to cut pumpkin because they can be super tough. If you're using a whole pumpkin, cut into quarters then scoop out the seeds with a fork or a smaller knife. Then cut into 3 cm cubes. If you have leftover pumpkin, it's perfect on toast for brekky the next morning! **Pair with:** Basil pesto and balsamic glaze.	**Time:** 7–8 minutes **Notes:** Don't throw away the seeds – these are amazing when baked in the oven with a pinch of salt. Use a sharp knife to cut pumpkin because it can be super tough. If you're using a whole pumpkin, cut into quarters then scoop out the seeds with a fork or a smaller knife. Then cut into 3 cm cubes. **Pair with:** Some lemony fish to balance out the gorgeous sweet taste of the pumpkin.
RADISH	**Time:** 18–20 minutes **Temperature:** 180°C **Notes:** Radish is a small, but spicy, vegetable. Roast them in halves. Poke a fork through and if slightly soft, they're ready! **Pair with:** A Thai-inspired salad.	**Time:** 10 minutes **Notes:** Poke a fork through the radish to ensure they're well-steamed. If slightly soft, they're ready! **Pair with:** Some people love radish with a little bit of butter, but I can't go past olive oil and a little lemon.
SWEET POTATO	**Time:** 35–40 minutes **Temperature:** 180°C **Notes:** My favourite way to season sweet potato is with Moroccan spice – a little seasoning can go a long way! The skin is great for fibre, so keep it on but give it a thorough wash. Slice into 2 cm thick circles. Once soft and lightly browned, they're ready! **Pair with:** Roasted beetroot to bulk up any boring salad – an awesome mix of colour and taste!	**Time:** 7–10 minutes **Notes:** Don't over-steam as it will become mushy. The skin is great for fibre, so keep it on but give it a thorough wash. Slice into 2 cm thick circles. Once soft, they're ready! **Pair with:** Some garlic, chives, salt and pepper to make my favourite sweet potato mash!
ZUCCHINI	**Time:** 15–20 minutes **Temperature:** 180°C **Notes:** Slice the zucchini lengthways or crossways, 2 cm thick. Then sprinkle with salt and squeeze out the excess water. If you leave them in for longer, they'll go a beautiful golden brown. **Pair with:** Eggplant! These two roast together perfectly.	**Time:** 3–5 minutes **Notes:** Slice the zucchini lengthways or crossways, 2 cm thick. Keep your eye on this veggie when steaming as they're already super watery. Steam for just a couple of minutes if you like a little bit of a crunch. **Pair with:** Olive oil, a squeeze of lemon, salt and pepper.

EGGS

Eggs are SUPER VERSATILE and one of my favourite protein sources. Ever popular for breakfast, they're also a great addition to savoury meals like fried rice, and a perfect binding ingredient for meatballs, baked goods and slices. I love trialling new ways to cook them because I believe that understanding different styles of cooking is the key to becoming a more inventive cook. It also helps make the cooking experience FUN and ENJOYABLE, as your meals will never be repetitive or boring. Learning how to poach, scramble and boil eggs will help you to expand your cooking repertoire and inspire you to think CREATIVELY in the kitchen.

BOILED

1. Place your eggs into a saucepan of boiling water with a pinch of salt.

2. Leave for your desired amount of time (see below), then drain and peel.

2 Minutes
Super soft (whites may still be runny)

4 Minutes
Soft-boiled

6 Minutes
Soft- to medium-boiled

POACHED

1. Heat water in a small saucepan over medium heat and bring to a simmer.

2. Add a teaspoon of salt. (There is no need for vinegar!)

3. Crack one egg into a small ramekin.

4. Use a spoon to create a light whirlpool in the water. Carefully drop the egg into the centre of the whirlpool – the water moving in one direction will prevent the egg from splitting in the pan.

5. Turn off the heat, cover with a lid and let it sit. Set a timer for 3–4 minutes for a soft-poached egg or 6–8 minutes for a hard-poached egg.

6. Scoop the egg out of the water using a slotted spoon. It's always best served immediately.

SCRAMBLED

1. Crack your eggs into a bowl and whisk. Add a splash of milk of your choice and continue whisking to combine.

2. Melt a tablespoon of butter or heat a splash of olive oil in a saucepan over low heat.

3. Pour the egg mixture into the pan and cook until it is set around the edges, about 1 minute.

4. Add fresh herbs like basil, parsley or chilli, or some grated cheese.

5. Using a spatula, stir to scramble by bringing the egg mixture from the outside of the pan into the centre. Continue this process until the eggs are cooked to your desired consistency.

8 Minutes
Medium- to hard-boiled

10 Minutes
Hard-boiled

Perfect scrambled eggs?
Have you ever made scrambled eggs that were super rubbery? This may be because you cooked them on a HIGH heat! Cooking eggs on a low heat will ensure they cook evenly without burning. You'll be left with super fluffy and delicious eggs.

CHICKEN

Like eggs, chicken is light and versatile – that's why people love it so much! It can be cooked in many different ways but most people tend to stick to the style they know and are confident with. But sticking to the one style can be dull. Here are my top tips on how to poach, pan-fry and roast chicken so that you're trying NEW and EXCITING ways to enjoy your favourite foods. Let's have some fun in the kitchen and give you an awesome cooking experience!

POACHED

1. Cut any excess fat off a chicken breast.

2. Fill a large saucepan with water and place the chicken in the bottom of the pan.

3. Place the pan over high heat and bring to the boil, then cover with a lid and turn the heat to low.

4. Lightly simmer for around 15 minutes or until the chicken is cooked through.

5. Cut the chicken breast in the thickest part to ensure it is completely white.

6. Remove the chicken from the pan and let it cool slightly before serving.

PAN-FRY

1. Coat a chicken breast or thigh with a teaspoon of olive oil, a teaspoon of dried oregano and salt and pepper. (This is my favourite seasoning but feel free to try your own!)

2. Heat a teaspoon of olive oil in a frying pan over medium–high heat.

3. Place the chicken in the pan and cook for around 7 minutes or until the edges are opaque. Try not to move the chicken until it is ready to turn over!

4. Turn over the chicken and fry for a further 7 minutes or until cooked through. Cut the chicken open to ensure there is absolutely no pink inside!

5. Rest for 5 minutes before serving.

ROAST

1. Coat the skin of a whole chicken with seasoning. Note: when you roast chicken, you always need seasoning as the chicken soaks up the flavour while it's cooking. My favourite seasoning is garlic, lemon, salt, pepper, dried oregano and maybe a little thyme. Play with flavours to see what suits you – just don't leave it plain!

2. Cover with plastic wrap and place in the fridge for at least 2 hours to marinate.

3. Preheat the oven to 210°C.

4. Transfer the chicken to a large baking dish. If you like, you can tie the legs together with kitchen twine but it isn't essential – it just helps hold the stuffing in if you are using it.

5. Place the chicken in the oven for 1 hour. Pierce the thickest part of the breast with a sharp knife and check the colour. If it's still pink, leave for an additional 5–10 minutes until cooked through.

6. Rest the chicken for 5–10 minutes before slicing.

BEEF

Beef can be cooked in many ways but my favourite way to cook it is on the barbecue. It's important to try different styles of cooking, so that you can change up your meals and make your diet more invigorating! I LOVE to trial, test, taste and create new things every day. But let's not make being creative hard; these are my top tips on how to cook the PERFECT pan-fried, roasted and chargrilled beef.

PAN-FRY

1. Heat a tablespoon of olive oil in a frying pan over medium–high heat.

2. Coat the steak with your favourite seasoning. Mine is garlic, salt, pepper and dried oregano!

3. Place the beef in the hot pan.

4. Each steak should be spaced evenly – if the pan is overcrowded the beef may stew and become tough.

5. Pan-fry to your liking. To test if cooked, lightly press the centre of the steak with tongs or your finger. If it's super soft, the steak is rare; if it's soft but springy, the steak is medium; if it's firm, the steak is well done!

6. Rest the steak for 5–10 minutes before serving.

ROAST

1. Preheat the oven to 200°C.

2. Coat a 500 g piece of beef (such as sirloin, tenderlion, rib roast or rump roast) with your favourite seasoning. Mine is olive oil, salt, pepper, garlic and dried oregano!

3. Place the beef in a baking dish with a splash of water or beef stock.

4. Roast for 25–35 minutes for a medium to well-done roast. (Note: increase the cooking time for larger pieces of beef. For example, cook 1 kg of beef for 1 hour.)

5. Remove the meat from the oven, cover loosely with foil and leave to rest for 10 minutes before serving.

BARBECUE OR CHARGRILL

1. Heat the barbecue to hot.

2. Lightly brush each steak with olive oil then sprinkle over your desired seasoning (If you haven't already guessed, mine is salt, pepper, garlic and dried oregano!).

3. Place the steaks on the barbecue and cook for 5–7 minutes on each side. To test if cooked, lightly press the centre of the steak with tongs or your finger. If it's super soft, the steak is rare; if it's soft but springy, the steak is medium; if it's firm, the steak is well done!

4. Remove from the barbecue, cover loosely with foil and leave to rest for a few minutes before serving.

DAY ON A PLATE

I've created these five 'days on a plate' to show you how my recipes can slot right into your day! The aim of this section is to give you inspiration for how to make your daily meals FUN and PRACTICAL and tailored to your needs. For example, do you need an energy lift? Try my ENERGY BOOST day on page 48. Is your immunity feeling a little low? Pick yourself up with my IMMUNITY ENHANCER day on page 50. All these plates are super EASY, TASTY and QUICK, meaning you won't be stuck in the kitchen for hours. Each day features a typical breakfast, lunch, dinner and snack that will provide the nutrients your body needs. Remember, these examples aren't restrictive and they can be changed to suit your lifestyle.

PAGE 201

LUNCH

Veggie Pasta Sauce
with Spaghetti

- DAY ON A PLATE -

VEGGIE PACKED

We should eat at least five servings of veggies and two servings of fruit every day. Today, you'll be eating the rainbow. Each meal has an abundance of fruit and veggies that your body will love you for!

PAGE 129

SNACK

Roast Pumpkin Hummus
with Veggie Sticks

PAGE 94

SNACK

Zucchini Slice

PAGE 75

BREAKFAST

Banana and Raspberry
Protein Pancakes

PAGE 209

DINNER

Stuffed Vegetables
with Quinoa

– DAY ON A PLATE –

ENERGY BOOST

Feeling a little low?
This day is absolutely packed with energy –
each meal will fuel your body for a busy day!

PAGE 81

DINNER

Beef and Brown Rice
Stir-fry

PAGE 123

LUNCH

Thai Beef
Noodle Salad

PAGE 83

BREAKFAST

Baked Eggs with Black Beans

PAGE 149

LUNCH

Ginger Chicken Meatballs
with Thai Salad

- DAY ON A PLATE -

♥

IMMUNITY ENHANCER

If you feel like you're about to catch a cold,
get these foods into you! Fuel yourself with
nutrient-dense food so your body
will fully recover.

- DAY ON A PLATE -

MEAL PREP ME

These meals are great for when we're super busy as they can be stored or prepped in advance. Meal prep doesn't have to be boring and bland – these are so delicious that you'll be eager for the next one!

PAGE 60

BREAKFAST

Granola

PAGE 128

SNACK

Roasted Beetroot and Feta Dip with Veggie Sticks

PAGE 178

LUNCH

Lemongrass Beef
Burrito Bowl

PAGE 174

DINNER

Pasta with Slow-cooked
Beef Ragu

PAGE 116

SNACK

Coconut Chilli
Bean Salad

- DAY ON A PLATE -
RESET

We sometimes get so caught up in life, that we forget to relax. Try taking it easy today with a light brekky, an easy lunch and a yummy dinner. Get out the movie marathon . . .

PAGE 120

LUNCH

Moroccan Chicken Salad

PAGE 97

SNACK

Zucchini and Pumpkin Fritters

PAGE 128

SNACK

Magic Guacamole with
Vegetable Sticks

PAGE 63

BREAKFAST

Berry Acai Bowl

PAGE 231

DINNER

Sweet Potato
and Lentil Patties

RECIPES

Big
BEAUTIFUL
♥
Breakfasts

GRANOLA

SERVES: 8
PREP TIME: 5 MINUTES
COOK TIME: 20 MINUTES

400 g (4 cups) rolled oats

40 g (¼ cup) almonds,
    coarsely crushed

30 g (¼ cup) pumpkin seeds

2 tablespoons chia seeds

30 g (¼ cup) sunflower seeds

45 g (¼ cup) dried
    apricots, chopped

30 g (¼ cup) dried cranberries

350 g (1 cup) warm honey

milk or yoghurt,
    to serve (optional)

Preheat the oven grill to 180°C. Line two large baking trays with baking paper.

Place the rolled oats, almonds, seeds and dried fruit in a large bowl and mix well. Pour over the warm honey and mix to coat evenly.

Divide the oat mixture between the prepared trays. Place a tray under the grill for 3 minutes. Remove the tray, stir the mixture and grill for another 3 minutes. Stir again and continue to grill in 1-minute intervals – checking to ensure the granola is not burning – until crunchy and golden brown, about 4 minutes. Set aside to cool. Repeat this process with the remaining oat mixture.

When both batches of granola are completely cool, place in an airtight container and store in the cupboard for up to 3 weeks.

Pair your granola with some milk or yoghurt.

Vegans can swap the honey for rice malt syrup.

BERRY ACAI BOWL

SERVES: 1
PREP TIME: 5 MINUTES

150 g (1 cup)
    frozen strawberries
1 frozen banana, chopped
2 tablespoons acai powder
250 ml (1 cup) almond milk
    (or milk of choice)
1 tablespoon nut butter

TOPPINGS
fresh fruit (such as berries,
    chopped banana,
    kiwi fruit, pineapple)
nuts and seeds
shredded coconut

Place the strawberries, banana, acai powder, milk and nut butter in a blender and blend until smooth. You don't want the mixture to be runny – aim for a frozen-yoghurt consistency.

Spoon the acai mixture into a bowl, top with your favourite fruit, nuts and seeds and sprinkle on the shredded coconut.

→ Acai is a berry from the acai palm tree, a native of Central and South America.

SIMPLE MUESLI

SERVES: 6
PREP TIME: 10 MINUTES
COOK TIME: 25 MINUTES

200 g (2 cups) rolled oats
60 g (½ cup) sunflower seeds
60 g (½ cup) slivered almonds
70 g (½ cup) pumpkin seeds
40 g (¼ cup) chia seeds

TO SERVE
yoghurt
fresh berries

Preheat the oven to 180°C. Line a large baking tray with baking paper.

Tip the rolled oats onto the prepared tray and spread out as much as you can. Place in the oven and toast for 3 minutes, or until the oats are lightly browned. Remove the tray from the oven and stir the oats with a spoon. Return the oats to the oven for a further 3 minutes, or until the oats are evenly light brown. Tip the oats into a large mixing bowl. Repeat this process with the sunflower seeds, almonds and pumpkin seeds.

Add the chia seeds to the toasted ingredients and mix well. Transfer the muesli to a large airtight jar and keep in a cool, dry place – like your cupboard – for up to 3 weeks.

Pair your muesli with some yoghurt and berries for a nutritious and filling breakfast.

Keep your eye on the rolled oats, seeds and almonds as you toast them – they can burn very easily.

OVERNIGHT BERRY OATS

SERVES: 1
PREP TIME: 5 MINUTES,
PLUS OVERNIGHT CHILLING

25 g (¼ cup) instant oats
  (you can use rolled oats, too)
125 ml (½ cup) almond milk
pinch of ground cinnamon
5–6 fresh raspberries
1 small handful of
  fresh blueberries
1 tablespoon shredded coconut
1 teaspoon honey

Mix all the ingredients in a bowl. Transfer to an airtight container and place in the fridge overnight.

In the morning, grab your berry oats and go.

 Vegans can swap out the honey for rice malt syrup.

OVERNIGHT SNICKERS OATS

SERVES: 1
PREP TIME: 5 MINUTES,
PLUS OVERNIGHT CHILLING

50 g (½ cup) instant oats
   (you can use rolled oats, too)
250 ml (1 cup) almond milk
1 tablespoon peanut butter
35 g chocolate whey
   protein powder
1 banana, finely sliced, plus
   extra to serve

Place all the ingredients in a bowl and mix well. Transfer to an airtight container and place in the fridge overnight.

In the morning, top with extra banana and enjoy.

Berry Bomb

Mango and Avocado

Coffee and Banana

SMOOTHIES

BERRY BOMB

VEGETARIAN · GLUTEN-FREE

SERVES: 2
PREP TIME: 5 MINUTES

150 g (1 cup)
   frozen strawberries
125 g (½ cup) Greek yoghurt
125 ml (½ cup) almond milk
30 g vanilla whey
   protein powder
fresh strawberries,
   to serve (optional)

Combine everything except fresh strawberries in a blender and blend until smooth.

Serve topped with strawberries (if using).

MANGO AND AVOCADO

VEGAN · GLUTEN-FREE

SERVES: 1
PREP TIME: 5 MINUTES

125 ml (½ cup) orange juice
125 ml (½ cup) coconut water
¼ avocado
½ teaspoon lime juice
150 g (1 cup) frozen diced mango
½ teaspoon flaxseed oil
lime, sliced, to serve (optional)

Combine everything except the lime slices in a blender and blend until smooth.

Serve with lime (if using).

Flaxseed oil has amazing omega-3 fatty acids that are great for healthy hearts, skin, hair and more.

BANANA AND COFFEE

VEGETARIAN · GLUTEN-FREE

SERVES: 1
PREP TIME: 5 MINUTES

1 frozen banana
30 g vanilla whey
   protein powder
1 shot of espresso coffee
250 ml (1 cup) almond milk
3 ice cubes
coffee beans, to
   serve (optional)

Combine everything except the coffee beans in a blender and blend until smooth.

Serve topped with coffee beans (if using).

Vegans can use pea protein powder or coconut yoghurt as a replacement for the whey protein powder.

BLUEBERRY MUFFINS

MAKES: 6
PREP TIME: 10 MINUTES
COOK TIME: 25 MINUTES

100 g (1 cup) almond meal
25 g (¼ cup) coconut flour
2 eggs
pinch of ground cinnamon
90 g (¼ cup) honey
3 very ripe bananas, mashed
125 g fresh blueberries

Preheat the oven to 180°C. Grease a 6-cup standard muffin tin.

Combine the almond meal, coconut flour, eggs, cinnamon, honey and banana in a bowl and mix thoroughly. Gently fold in the blueberries.

Spoon the muffin mixture into the prepared tin and bake in the oven for 25 minutes, or until the muffins are lightly browned. To test if they are cooked through, stick a skewer in the middle of a muffin – if it comes out clean, they're ready.

*Don't like blueberries?
Try raspberries or diced apple.*

BANANA *and* RASPBERRY PROTEIN PANCAKES

SERVES: 2
PREP TIME: 10 MINUTES
COOK TIME: 10 MINUTES

3 very ripe large
   bananas, mashed
60 g vanilla whey
   protein powder
2 eggs
butter or coconut oil,
   for frying
60 g (½ cup) fresh raspberries

TO SERVE
Greek yoghurt
honey

Combine the banana, protein powder and eggs in a large bowl and mix thoroughly. The mixture will seem runny but that is OK.

Melt a tablespoon of butter or coconut oil in a frying pan over low heat. Spoon 3 tablespoons of batter per pancake into the pan and cook, three pancakes per batch, for 3 minutes, or until bubbles form on the surface. Alternatively, if you like raspberries in your batter, spoon 3 tablespoons of batter per pancake into the pan, scatter over a small handful of raspberries and cook, three pancakes per batch, for 3 minutes, or until bubbles form on the surface.

Flip the pancake and cook for a further 2 minutes, or until the underside is golden brown. Repeat with the remaining batter so you have six pancakes in total.

Top each pancake with some Greek yoghurt, raspberries and honey and serve.

Don't like raspberries?
Swap for blueberries.

QUINOA PANCAKES

MAKES: 8
PREP TIME: 5 MINUTES
COOK TIME: 40 MINUTES

150 g (1 cup) wholemeal
    plain flour

100 g (1 cup) quinoa flakes

375 ml (1½ cups) almond milk

2 eggs, lightly whisked

1 teaspoon LSA (flaxseeds,
    sunflower seeds
    and almonds)

1 banana, mashed

2 tablespoons honey,
    plus extra to serve

pinch of ground cinnamon

butter or coconut oil, for frying

fresh fruit, to serve

Place the flour, quinoa flakes, milk, eggs, LSA, banana, honey and cinnamon in a bowl and mix well.

Melt the butter or coconut oil in a frying pan over medium heat. Pour in about ½ cup of batter and tilt the pan so the batter spreads to form a disc. Cook for 3 minutes, or until bubbles appear on the surface of the pancake. Turn and cook for a further 2 minutes, or until golden on the underside. Remove and place on a warm plate. Repeat with the remaining batter until you have eight pancakes in total.

Once all your pancakes are cooked, serve them with your choice of fruit and a drizzle of honey.

Use coconut oil instead of butter to keep your pancakes dairy-free!

SPICY SCRAMBLED TOFU

SERVES: 1
PREP TIME: 10 MINUTES
COOK TIME: 10 MINUTES

¼ teaspoon smoked paprika

¼ teaspoon ground cumin

¼ teaspoon ground turmeric

½ teaspoon garlic powder

olive oil, for frying

1 spring onion, finely sliced

150 g extra-firm tofu, drained

5 cherry tomatoes

¼ avocado, diced

pinch of freshly ground
    black pepper

1 slice of rye bread, toasted

To prepare the seasoning, in a small bowl, mix together the paprika, cumin, turmeric and garlic powder.

Heat a little olive oil in a small non-stick frying pan over medium heat. Add the spring onion and cook for 1 minute, or until softened.

Using your fingers, break the tofu into small pieces and crumble into the pan. Sprinkle the seasoning over the tofu and mix well.

Add the cherry tomatoes and avocado to the spiced tofu mixture and cook, stirring occasionally, for 5 minutes, or until the tomatoes begin to burst. Add a sprinkle of pepper and stir for another 2 minutes.

Serve the scrambled tofu with the toasted rye and your morning coffee, if you like!

Tofu is an excellent food from a nutritional and health perspective. Abundant with amino acids, iron and calcium, it's the most popular source of protein for vegans and vegetarians.

SMOKED SALMON
on RYE

SERVES: 2
PREP TIME: 10 MINUTES

100 g cream cheese, softened
1 tablespoon baby capers
¼ red onion, finely diced
1 teaspoon finely grated
   lemon zest
1 tablespoon lemon juice
4 slices of rye bread, toasted
   (or rye crackers)
100 g smoked salmon,
   finely sliced
1 tablespoon finely
   chopped chives

Place the cream cheese in a bowl. Add the capers, onion, lemon zest and juice and mix thoroughly.

Smear the cream cheese mixture on the toasted rye, arrange the smoked salmon on top and scatter over the chives.

BAKED EGGS
with BLACK BEANS

SERVES: 2
PREP TIME: 15 MINUTES
COOK TIME: 20–25 MINUTES

1 tablespoon olive oil

½ onion, finely diced

1 garlic clove, crushed

1 × 400 g can whole
  peeled tomatoes

100 g canned, drained
  black beans

½ teaspoon dried oregano

½ teaspoon chilli flakes (add
  more if you like it extra hot)

pinch each of salt flakes and
  freshly ground black pepper

4 eggs

2 tablespoons grated parmesan

Preheat the oven to 180°C.

Heat the olive oil in a saucepan over medium heat, add the onion and garlic and fry, stirring occasionally, for 5 minutes, or until the onion is softened. Stir in the tomatoes, black beans, oregano, chilli flakes and salt and pepper and simmer for 5 minutes.

Spoon 1 tablespoon of the tomato mixture into the base of two 2-cup capacity ovenproof bowls. Crack 2 eggs into each bowl, then cover with the rest of the tomato mixture. Sprinkle the parmesan over the top and bake in the oven for 10 minutes (for runny eggs) or 15 minutes (for medium–well-done eggs).

Try to use free-range eggs, as that typically means 1500 hens per hectare. Some free-range companies have 200–300 hens per hectare – and that is even better. Aim for the lowest number of chickens per hectare.

BASIL *and* CHERRY TOMATO OMELETTE

SERVES: 1
PREP TIME: 5 MINUTES
COOK TIME: 10 MINUTES

1 tablespoon olive oil
6 cherry tomatoes, halved
3 basil leaves, plus extra
   to serve
salt flakes and freshly ground
   black pepper
3 eggs, whisked
1 slice of rye bread, toasted
¼ avocado, finely sliced

Heat the olive oil in a frying pan over medium heat, add the tomatoes and cook for 4 minutes, or until the tomatoes begin to burst.

Scatter the basil leaves and sprinkle salt and pepper over the tomatoes. Pour the eggs into the pan and cook for 2 minutes, or until the eggs are set on the underside. Flip and cook for a further minute, or until the eggs are just set.

Serve the omelette with the rye toast and avocado and scatter over some extra basil leaves.

CHILLI SCRAMBLED EGGS *with* ASPARAGUS *and* SUNDRIED TOMATOES

SERVES: 1
PREP TIME: 5 MINUTES
COOK TIME: 10 MINUTES

1 tablespoon butter
2 asparagus spears, woody
   ends trimmed, cut into
   2.5 cm lengths
½ small red chilli, deseeded
   and finely sliced
1 spring onion, finely sliced
5 sun-dried tomatoes, halved
3 eggs, whisked
herbs (such as coriander,
   parsley or basil leaves)
   or dukkah, to serve
1 slice of rye bread,
   toasted (optional)

Melt the butter in a small saucepan over medium heat. Add the asparagus, chilli, spring onion and sun-dried tomatoes and cook for 3 minutes, or until the asparagus is just tender.

Pour the eggs into the pan and cook until set around the edge, about 30 seconds. Stir to scramble, bringing the egg mixture from the outside of the pan into the centre. Leave to cook for another 30 seconds or so and stir again. Continue this process until the eggs are just set, about 3 minutes.

Spoon your scrambled eggs onto a warm plate, scatter over the herbs or dukkah and serve with the rye toast (if using).

SMOKED SALMON *with* EGGS, AVOCADO *and* DUKKAH

SERVES: 1
PREP TIME: 10 MINUTES
COOK TIME: 10 MINUTES

½ avocado, mashed

1 tablespoon lemon juice

pinch of salt flakes and freshly
    ground black pepper

1 tablespoon olive oil

3–4 asparagus spears, woody
    ends trimmed

1 slice of sourdough bread

2 poached eggs (page 37)

50 g smoked salmon

1 tablespoon spicy dukkah

Combine the avocado, lemon juice and salt and pepper
in a small bowl.

Heat the olive oil in a small frying pan over medium heat,
add the asparagus and fry, turning occasionally, until just
tender, about 3 minutes.

Place the bread in the toaster and start poaching
your eggs.

Spread the avocado mixture over the toast and top with
the asparagus, smoked salmon and eggs. Sprinkle over
the dukkah and you're set for an amazing breakfast.

Mushroom and Ham

Capsicum, Leek and Parmesan

~ 2 WAYS ~
FRITTATA

MUSHROOM AND HAM

GLUTEN-FREE

SERVES: 4
PREP TIME: 10 MINUTES
COOK TIME: 35 MINUTES

1 tablespoon butter

½ onion, diced

1 garlic clove, crushed

200 g double smoked ham, finely chopped

10 button mushrooms, cleaned and finely sliced

2 vine-ripened tomatoes, diced

90 g (2 cups) baby spinach leaves

10 eggs, whisked

100 g feta, crumbled

salt flakes and freshly ground black pepper,
    to taste

Preheat the oven to 180°C. Grease a 22 cm round baking dish.

Melt the butter in a frying pan over medium heat, add the onion, garlic, ham and mushrooms and cook, stirring occasionally, for 5 minutes, or until the onion is softened.

Add the tomato and spinach to the pan and cook until the spinach is wilted, about 1 minute.

Spoon the onion mixture into the prepared dish. Pour the whisked eggs over the top and gently stir to combine. Scatter over the feta and season with salt and pepper. Bake in the oven for 25 minutes, or until puffed and golden on top.

Pair your frittata with yummy Basil Pesto (page 113) and you've got yourself a winner brekky.

CAPSICUM, LEEK AND PARMESAN

VEGETARIAN · GLUTEN-FREE

SERVES: 4
PREP TIME: 10 MINUTES
COOK TIME: 35 MINUTES

2 tablespoons butter

2 leeks, white and light green parts only,
    washed and finely sliced

2 garlic cloves, crushed

1 tablespoon chopped thyme leaves

1 handful of roughly chopped flat-leaf parsley

200 g roasted red capsicum, finely sliced

10 eggs

50 g (½ cup) grated parmesan

salt flakes and freshly ground black pepper,
    to taste

Preheat the oven to 180°C. Grease a 22 cm round baking dish.

Melt the butter in a frying pan over medium heat, add the leek, garlic, thyme and parsley and cook, stirring occasionally, for 5 minutes, or until the leek is softened. Stir in the capsicum and cook for a further 2 minutes.

Crack the eggs into a bowl and whisk. Add the parmesan and season with salt and pepper.

Spoon the leek mixture into the prepared dish, pour the egg mixture over the top and gently stir to combine. Bake in the oven for 25 minutes, or until puffed and golden on top.

ZUCCHINI SLICE

SERVES: 4
PREP TIME: 15 MINUTES
COOK TIME: 30 MINUTES

3 zucchini, ends trimmed

½ red capsicum, diced

4–6 button mushrooms, cleaned and finely sliced

1 onion, diced

1 garlic clove, crushed

1 handful of chopped flat-leaf parsley

50 g (⅓ cup) grated mozzarella cheese

5 eggs

150 g (1 cup) self-raising flour

1 teaspoon each of salt flakes and freshly ground black pepper

Preheat the oven to 180°C. Line a 22 × 33 cm baking tin with baking paper.

Coarsely grate the zucchini into a clean Chux cloth, then squeeze to remove as much liquid as possible (this is important – you don't want your slice to be watery).

Combine the vegetables, garlic and parsley in a large bowl. Add the cheese, eggs, flour, salt and pepper and mix thoroughly.

Spoon the zucchini mixture into the lined tin, smooth the surface and bake in the oven for 30 minutes, or until lightly browned on top. Serve hot or cold.

My favourite way to enjoy this slice is cold – it's a perfect 3 o'clock snack when you start to get those cravings.

ZUCCHINI and PUMPKIN FRITTERS

MAKES: 40
PREP TIME: 15 MINUTES
COOK TIME: 25 MINUTES

3 zucchini, roughly chopped

1 small carrot, roughly chopped

300 g (2 cups) diced
    butternut pumpkin

2 onions, roughly chopped

1 garlic clove, crushed

1 handful of flat-leaf
    parsley leaves, plus extra
    to serve (optional)

1 handful of mint leaves, plus
    extra to serve (optional)

2 eggs

100 g (1 cup) dry breadcrumbs,
    plus extra if needed

100 g (⅔ cup) self-raising flour

½ teaspoon each of salt
    flakes and freshly ground
    black pepper

100 g feta

olive oil, for frying

Lime Aioli (page 138),
    to serve (optional)

Place the zucchini in a food processor and process into small pieces. Transfer to a clean Chux cloth and squeeze to remove as much liquid as possible (this step is important so the fritters don't become soggy).

Add the carrot, pumpkin, onion, garlic, parsley and mint to the food processor and process until finely chopped.

Place the vegetable mixture and the zucchini in a large bowl and add the eggs, breadcrumbs, flour and salt and pepper. Mix thoroughly and add more breadcrumbs if the mixture is too wet. Crumble in the feta and mix well. Take 1 tablespoon of mixture at a time and shape into small patties.

Heat the olive oil in a large frying pan over medium heat. Add the fritters in batches of ten and cook for 2–3 minutes on each side until lightly browned.

Serve hot or cold either by themselves or with some delicious lime aioli and scatter over mint and parsley leaves (if using).

These are perfect as an appetiser at a party.

SWEET POTATO CHIPS
with SPICY MAYO

SERVES: 3
PREP TIME: 10 MINUTES
COOK TIME: 40 MINUTES

1 teaspoon salt flakes

1 teaspoon dried oregano

1 teaspoon chilli powder

½ teaspoon ground turmeric

1 teaspoon garlic powder

1 teaspoon smoked paprika

2 sweet potatoes, cut into long
     thin strips (French-fry style)

2 tablespoons olive oil

SPICY MAYO

80 g whole egg mayonnaise

¼ teaspoon hot sauce

squeeze of lime juice

Preheat the oven to 180°C. Line a large baking tray
with baking paper.

Combine the dried herbs and spices in a small bowl
and mix well.

Place the sweet potato in a large bowl, drizzle over the
oil and toss to coat. Add the spice mix and toss again
to coat evenly.

Spread the spiced sweet potato chips on the lined tray.
Roast in the oven for 40 minutes, or until the chips are
golden brown and cooked through.

For the spicy mayo, combine the mayo, hot sauce and
lime juice in a small bowl and mix well.

Dip the sweet potato chips in the spicy mayo and enjoy.

PESTO PASTA SALAD

SERVES: 4
PREP TIME: 10 MINUTES

250 g cherry tomatoes, halved
80 g (½ cup) pitted
    kalamata olives
½ Lebanese cucumber,
    cut into small pieces
3 marinated artichoke hearts,
    drained and quartered
250 g cooked spiral pasta
80 g Basil Pesto (page 113),
    plus extra if needed
salt flakes and freshly ground
    black pepper, to taste
basil leaves, to serve (optional)

Place the cherry tomatoes, olives, cucumber and artichoke hearts in a large bowl. Throw in the cooked pasta and spoon on the pesto. Mix thoroughly, ensuring all the pasta is covered. If necessary, add more pesto. Scatter over basil leaves (if using) and season with a little salt and pepper and eat.

BEAN SALAD

SERVES: 4
PREP TIME: 15 MINUTES

1 × 750 g can four bean mix
10 cherry tomatoes, halved
1 Lebanese cucumber, diced
½ avocado, diced
½ red onion, finely diced
½ red capsicum, finely diced
1 small handful of roughly
   chopped flat-leaf parsley
1 tablespoon olive oil
1 tablespoon lemon juice
salt flakes and freshly ground
   black pepper, to taste

Combine the bean mix, cherry tomatoes, cucumber, avocado, onion, capsicum and parsley in a large bowl and drizzle over the olive oil and lemon juice. Sprinkle on some salt and pepper and serve. This salad will keep, stored in an airtight container, in the fridge for up to 3 days.

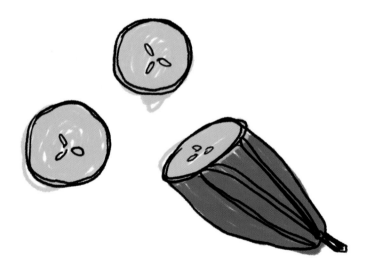

GREEK SALAD

SERVES: 1
PREP TIME: 10 MINUTES

**2 teaspoons extra-virgin
  olive oil**
juice of ½ lemon
pinch of dried oregano
**salt flakes and freshly ground
  black pepper**
**2 tomatoes, cut into
  thin wedges**
**1 Lebanese cucumber,
  cut into thin strips**
½ red onion, finely sliced
**½ green capsicum, cut into
  thin strips**
**60 g feta (or 10 times that
  if you love feta!)**

To make the dressing, in a small bowl, combine the olive oil, lemon juice and oregano, sprinkle in salt and pepper and mix well.

Place the tomato, cucumber, onion and capsicum in a separate bowl and crumble the feta over the top. Pour on the dressing, toss well and serve.

CHARGRILLED SQUID SALAD

SERVES: 2
PREP TIME: 15 MINUTES
COOK TIME: 5 MINUTES

1 tablespoon olive oil
250 g cleaned squid tubes,
    cut into 5 mm thick rings
pinch of salt flakes and freshly
    ground black pepper
juice of ½ lemon
½ savoy cabbage, finely sliced
1 Lebanese cucumber, peeled
    and cut into thin strips using
    a mandoline
1 red onion, finely sliced
1 long red chilli, deseeded
    and finely sliced
3 radishes, finely sliced
1 carrot, cut into thin strips
    using a mandoline
1 handful of roughly
    chopped mint
1 handful of roughly chopped
    coriander leaves
1 tablespoon fish sauce
2 teaspoons sesame oil
1 teaspoon brown sugar
juice of 1 lime

Drizzle the olive oil over the squid rings and sprinkle with a pinch of salt and pepper.

Heat a barbecue flat plate to medium and cook the squid rings for 4 minutes, or until they turn white. Take them off the heat and squeeze over the lemon juice.

Place the cabbage, cucumber, onion, chilli, radish, carrot, mint and coriander in a large bowl.

Combine the fish sauce, sesame oil, brown sugar and lime juice in a small bowl, mix well and pour over the salad.

Add the squid to the dressed salad and toss. Evenly divide between serving plates or bowls and eat straightaway.

ROAST VEGETABLE WRAPS

SERVES: 4
PREP TIME: 15 MINUTES
COOK TIME: 30 MINUTES

220 g butternut
    pumpkin, peeled and
    deseeded, chopped into
    bite-sized pieces
1 zucchini, finely
    sliced lengthways
1 eggplant, finely
    sliced lengthways
10 button mushrooms,
    cleaned and quartered
2 beetroot, sliced into
    thin rounds
1 red capsicum, finely
    sliced (optional)
olive oil, for drizzling
salt flakes and freshly ground
    black pepper
75 g (⅓ cup) hummus
4 rye wraps
3 handfuls of rocket leaves

Preheat the oven to 200°C. Line a large baking tray with baking paper.

Spread all the vegetables on the lined tray. Drizzle on a generous amount of olive oil and sprinkle with salt and pepper. Roast for 30 minutes, or until the vegetables are slightly charred.

Spoon a quarter of the hummus into the middle of each wrap. Layer each veggie on top and add a handful of rocket. Wrap up and eat straightaway.

➡️ *Don't buy your hummus, DIY with the recipe on page 226.*

ROAST VEGGIE SALAD *with* SPICY AVOCADO DRESSING

SERVES: 2
PREP TIME: 15 MINUTES
COOK TIME: 40 MINUTES

1 red capsicum, thickly sliced

5 button mushrooms,
    cleaned and halved

155 g butternut
    pumpkin, peeled and
    deseeded, chopped into
    bite-sized pieces

1 zucchini, cut into 1 cm rounds

olive oil, for drizzling

pinch of salt flakes and freshly
    ground black pepper

1 handful of rocket leaves

1 handful of baby spinach leaves

SPICY AVOCADO DRESSING

1 avocado

1 garlic clove, crushed

1 small jalapeno chilli, deseeded

¼ teaspoon chilli flakes

1 teaspoon ground cumin

2 tablespoons lemon juice

2 tablespoons extra-virgin
    olive oil

Preheat the oven to 180°C. Line a baking tray with baking paper.

Spread the capsicum, mushrooms, pumpkin and zucchini on the lined tray, drizzle over the olive oil, sprinkle on some salt and pepper and roast in the oven for 40 minutes, or until the vegetables are tender.

To make the dressing, combine the avocado, garlic, jalapeno, chilli flakes, cumin, lemon juice, olive oil and a sprinkle of salt and pepper in a blender and whiz until smooth. Add 2 tablespoons of water and blend again.

Place the rocket and spinach in two serving bowls, add the vegetables and serve with the avocado dressing on the side.

HALOUMI and ROAST VEGGIE SALAD

SERVES: 2
PREP TIME: 10 MINUTES
COOK TIME: 40 MINUTES

1 large beetroot,
    cut into wedges
300 g butternut
    pumpkin, peeled and
    deseeded, chopped into
    bite-sized pieces
3 tablespoons olive oil
1 teaspoon dried oregano
1 teaspoon smoked
    paprika (optional)
¼ teaspoon chilli
    flakes (optional)
250 g cherry tomatoes
200 g haloumi, cut into
    2 cm cubes
1 tablespoon lemon juice
185 g (1 cup) cooked long-grain
    brown rice
2 handfuls of rocket leaves
2 tablespoons pine nuts, toasted

BASIL PESTO
(MAKES 375 G [½ CUPS])
100 g (2 cups, tightly packed)
    basil leaves
50 g (⅓ cup) pine nuts, toasted
125 ml (½ cup) extra-virgin
    olive oil
3 garlic cloves, crushed
salt flakes and freshly ground
    black pepper, to taste
1 tablespoon lemon juice

To make the basil pesto, place all the pesto ingredients in a food processor and whiz. I like mine a little chunky but the consistency is up to you.

Preheat the oven to 180°C. Line a baking tray with baking paper.

Spread the beetroot and pumpkin on the lined tray, drizzle over 2 tablespoons of the olive oil, sprinkle on the dried oregano and a little salt and pepper. If you want a little spice, now's the time to chuck on the paprika or chilli flakes. Roast in the oven for 20 minutes. Throw in the cherry tomatoes and roast for a further 10–15 minutes until the vegetables are tender and the tomatoes are bursting out of their skins.

Meanwhile, splash the remaining olive oil into a frying pan and heat over medium heat. Add the haloumi and fry, stirring occasionally, until golden brown, about 4 minutes. Remove from the pan and squeeze the lemon juice over the top.

Divide the brown rice, roast veggies, rocket and haloumi between two serving bowls, dollop on a couple of tablespoons of basil pesto, mix through and scatter over the pine nuts.

→ *Pesto is great because it's super versatile. Make a batch and keep in an airtight container in the fridge for up to 2 weeks.*

COUSCOUS *and* ROAST VEGETABLE SALAD

SERVES: 2
PREP TIME: 20 MINUTES
COOK TIME: 40 MINUTES

150 g butternut
    pumpkin, peeled and
    deseeded, chopped into
    bite-sized pieces
1 large red capsicum
1½ tablespoons olive oil
salt flakes and freshly ground
    black pepper
60 g (⅓ cup) couscous
170 ml (⅔ cup) boiling water
juice of 1 lemon
1 teaspoon red wine vinegar
1 red onion, finely diced
2 tomatoes, diced
1 small red chilli, deseeded
    and finely chopped
2 tablespoons basil leaves
2 tablespoons coriander leaves

Preheat the oven to 180°C. Line a baking tray with baking paper.

Place the pumpkin and capsicum in a bowl, splash on 1 tablespoon of the olive oil and sprinkle on some salt and pepper. Transfer to the lined tray and roast in the oven for 20 minutes. Turn the capsicum over, give the pumpkin a stir and roast for a further 20 minutes, or until the pumpkin is tender and the capsicum is collapsed and charred.

Place the capsicum in a small bowl, cover with plastic wrap and leave to steam for 5 minutes. Peel and deseed the capsicum, then chop into tiny pieces.

Meanwhile, place the couscous in a bowl, pour over the boiling water, cover with plastic wrap and a tea towel and set aside to steam for 10 minutes.

Fluff the couscous with a fork, add the lemon juice and a sprinkle of salt and pepper. Drizzle over the red wine vinegar and the remaining olive oil and mix through. Add the onion, tomato, chilli and herbs and gently mix. Scatter over the roasted capsicum and pumpkin, mix again and serve.

COCONUT CHILLI BEAN SALAD

SERVES: 4
PREP TIME: 10 MINUTES
COOK TIME: 5 MINUTES

**400 g green beans, topped
    and tailed**
½ red onion, finely sliced
15 g (¼ cup) shredded coconut
**roasted peanuts, crushed,
    to serve**

DRESSING
1 tablespoon sesame oil
1 tablespoon tamari
2 tablespoons rice vinegar
zest and juice of 1 lime
**1 small red chilli, deseeded
    and finely chopped**
1 garlic clove, crushed
1 tablespoon brown sugar

Steam or blanch the beans until just tender.

To make the dressing, combine the sesame oil, tamari, rice vinegar, lime zest and juice, chilli, garlic and brown sugar in a small bowl and mix well.

Place the beans and onion in a large bowl, add three-quarters of the dressing and gently toss to coat. If you think the salad needs more, add the rest of the dressing. If you don't use the rest of the dressing, store in an airtight container in the fridge for up to a week.

Scatter the shredded coconut and peanuts over the top and serve.

The leftover dressing is delicious on veggies. Check out pages 30–34 for the perfect way to steam your veggies.

FENNEL SALAD

SERVES: 4
PREP TIME: 10 MINUTES

1 large fennel bulb,
    finely sliced
1 orange, peeled and
    finely sliced, crossways
    into rounds
1 large handful of roughly
    chopped flat-leaf parsley
fennel fronds,
    to serve (optional)

DRESSING
juice of ½ orange
juice of ½ lemon
¼ teaspoon salt flakes
2 teaspoons extra-virgin
    olive oil

To make the dressing, in a small bowl, combine the orange and lemon juices, salt and olive oil and whisk well.

Place the fennel, orange slices and parsley in a large bowl and mix well. Add half the dressing and gently toss. If you want more dressing, add as you wish. If you don't use the rest of the dressing, store in an airtight container in the fridge for up to a week.

Scatter over fennel fronds (if using) and serve.

MOROCCAN CHICKEN SALAD

SERVES: 2
PREP TIME: 15 MINUTES
COOK TIME: 40 MINUTES

1 chicken breast fillet,
    cut into thin strips
3 tablespoons Moroccan
    spice mix
150 g butternut
    pumpkin, peeled and
    deseeded, chopped into
    bite-sized pieces
1 tablespoon olive oil
2 tablespoons extra-virgin
    olive oil
1 large handful of mixed salad
    leaves, finely sliced
45 g (¼ cup) stuffed
    green olives
35 g (¼ cup) sun-dried
    tomatoes, halved
1 handful of alfalfa sprouts
60 g feta, crumbled
juice of ½ lemon
pinch of salt flakes

Preheat the oven to 200°C. Line a baking tray with baking paper.

Place the chicken strips in a bowl, add 2 tablespoons of the Moroccan spice mix and toss to coat. Set aside.

Combine the pumpkin, olive oil and the remaining Moroccan spice mix in a bowl and toss well. Transfer to the lined tray and bake in the oven for 30 minutes, or until the pumpkin is tender.

Heat 1 tablespoon of the extra-virgin olive oil in a large frying pan over medium heat, add the chicken in small batches and cook, stirring occasionally, until completely cooked through.

Place the salad leaves, olives, sun-dried tomatoes, alfalfa and feta in a salad bowl and gently mix. Add the chicken and pumpkin and gently toss to combine. Drizzle the lemon juice and remaining extra-virgin olive oil over the top and sprinkle on the salt. Mix again and serve.

THAI BEEF NOODLE SALAD

SERVES: 4 • PREP TIME: 15 MINUTES, PLUS 1 HOUR MARINATING
COOK TIME: 20 MINUTES

---

300 g beef tenderloins, cut into thin strips

MARINADE
1 small red chilli, deseeded and finely chopped
juice of 1 lime
2 tablespoons oyster sauce
2 tablespoons soy sauce
2 garlic cloves, crushed

DRESSING
juice of ½ lime
1 tablespoon fish sauce
1 tablespoon sesame oil
1 small red chilli, deseeded and finely chopped
1 tablespoon roughly chopped mint
1 tablespoon roughly chopped coriander leaves
1 teaspoon soy sauce

SALAD
250 g rice noodles, cooked according to packet instructions
50 g fried noodles
1 red capsicum, finely sliced
1 large cucumber, finely sliced
1 red onion, finely sliced
¼ Chinese cabbage (wong bok), finely sliced
2 carrots, finely sliced
1 handful of roughly chopped mint
1 handful of roughly chopped coriander leaves

Combine all the marinade ingredients in a bowl and mix well. Add the beef strips and toss to coat. Cover with plastic wrap and place in the fridge for 1 hour to really bring out the flavours.

Place all the dressing ingredients in a bowl and stir to combine. Set aside.

Combine all the salad ingredients in a large bowl and mix thoroughly.

Heat a non-stick frying pan over high heat, add the beef in small batches (if you crowd the pan, you'll end up with tough strips of meat) and stir-fry for 5 minutes or until just cooked through.

Tip the beef onto the salad and pour the dressing over the top. Toss and divide among four serving bowls.

SWEET POTATO
and PUMPKIN SOUP

SERVES: 6
PREP TIME: 10 MINUTES
COOK TIME: 50 MINUTES

1 tablespoon olive oil

1 onion, quartered

500 g butternut pumpkin,
   peeled and deseeded,
   roughly chopped

500 g sweet potato,
   roughly chopped

200 g desiree potatoes,
   roughly chopped

2 garlic cloves, crushed

1.5 litres (6 cups)
   vegetable stock

1 teaspoon ground cumin

1 teaspoon each of salt
   flakes and freshly ground
   black pepper

1 tablespoon roughly chopped
   coriander leaves

Splash the olive oil into a large saucepan and heat over high heat. Add the vegetables and cook, stirring occasionally, for 4 minutes, or until the onion is softened. Stir in the garlic, then pour in the vegetable stock and bring to a simmer, about 5 minutes.

Add the cumin, salt and pepper to the pan and simmer for 40 minutes, or until the vegetables are super soft. Use a hand-held blender to puree the soup until smooth. Top with the coriander, sprinkle with pepper and serve.

- 4 WAYS -
DIPS

Roast Capsicum and Semi-dried Tomato Oil
(page 129)

Magic Guacamole
(page 128)

Roast Beetroot
and Feta Dip
(page 128)

Roast Pumpkin Hummus
(page 129)

seedy crackers
(page 136)

- 4 WAYS -
DIPS

MAGIC GUACAMOLE

VEGAN · GLUTEN-FREE

MAKES: ABOUT 230 G (1 CUP)
PREP TIME: 5 MINUTES

2 avocados, sliced

½ red onion, grated

juice of ½ lemon

1 small garlic clove, crushed

**pinch of salt flakes and freshly
  ground black pepper**

**veggie sticks or Seedy Crackers (page 136),
  to serve**

Place the avocado in a bowl and mash. Add all the other ingredients and mix to form a smooth paste (or leave it chunky if you like).

Spoon into a serving bowl and serve with some yummy veggies or crackers.

ROAST BEETROOT AND FETA DIP

VEGETARIAN · GLUTEN-FREE

MAKES: 400 G (1½ CUPS)
PREP TIME: 10 MINUTES
COOK TIME: 40 MINUTES

**500 g beetroot, peeled and chopped
  into wedges**

olive oil, for drizzling

1 garlic clove, crushed

30 g (¼ cup) walnuts

65 g Danish feta

**veggie sticks or Seedy Crackers (page 136),
  to serve**

Preheat the oven to 180°C. Line a baking tray with baking paper.

Spread the beetroot on the lined tray, drizzle over some olive oil and roast in the oven for 30–40 minutes until tender. Set aside to cool.

Place the beetroot, garlic, walnuts and feta in a food processor and pulse until chunky but combined. Leave it a little chunky or continue to pulse if you prefer a smoother dip.

Spoon into a serving bowl and serve with some yummy veggies or crackers.

Wear plastic food-handling gloves while peeling the beetroot or you'll have ruby-red hands. ←

ROAST CAPSICUM AND SEMI-DRIED TOMATO DIP

VEGETARIAN · GLUTEN-FREE

MAKES: 375 G (1 ½ CUPS)
PREP TIME: 10 MINUTES
COOK TIME: 25 MINUTES

750 g red capsicums (about 3 large),
    halved lengthways and deseeded
150 g semi-dried tomatoes
1 garlic clove, crushed
1 tablespoon grated parmesan
1 small dried red chilli
6 basil leaves
sprinkle of salt flakes and freshly
    ground black pepper
3 tablespoons olive oil
veggie sticks or Seedy Crackers (page 136),
    to serve

Preheat the grill to 200°C. Line a baking tray with baking paper.

Arrange the capsicum pieces, skin-side up, on the lined tray and grill for 15 minutes, or until blackened and soft. (Don't stress about the black bits, they will come off.) Place the capsicum in a plastic bag and seal to ensure no air escapes. Leave to steam for 10 minutes.

When the capsicum is cool enough to handle, peel and discard the skin, then place the flesh in a food processor. Add the semi-dried tomatoes, garlic, parmesan, chilli, basil and salt and pepper and whiz to combine. While blending, slowly drizzle in the olive oil and process to a paste.

Spoon into a serving bowl and serve with some yummy veggies or crackers.

ROAST PUMPKIN HUMMUS

VEGAN · GLUTEN-FREE

MAKES: 440 G (2 CUPS)
PREP TIME: 15 MINUTES
COOK TIME: 40 MINUTES

700 g butternut pumpkin, peeled and deseeded,
    chopped into bite-sized pieces
olive oil, for drizzling
salt flakes and freshly ground black pepper
1 × 400 g can chickpeas, rinsed and drained
1 tablespoon hulled tahini
juice of ½ lemon
1 garlic clove, crushed
1 small dried red chilli
2 tablespoons coriander leaves
veggie sticks or Seedy Crackers (page 136),
    to serve

Preheat the oven to 180°C. Line a baking tray with baking paper.

Spread the pumpkin on the lined tray, drizzle over a small amount of olive oil and sprinkle on some salt and pepper. Roast in the oven for 40 minutes, or until the pumpkin is tender. Allow to cool.

Combine the pumpkin, chickpeas, tahini, lemon juice, garlic, chilli and coriander in a food processor and process to your desired consistency. Season with a little more salt and pepper.

Spoon into a serving bowl and serve with some yummy veggies or crackers.

VANILLA CHIA-SEED PUDDING

SERVES: 4
PREP TIME: 10 MINUTES,
PLUS OVERNIGHT TO SET

185 ml (¾ cup) milk of choice

250 g (1 cup) Greek yoghurt

2 tablespoons honey

½ teaspoon natural
    vanilla extract

40 g (¼ cup) chia seeds

TOPPING IDEAS
fresh berries
sliced banana
Granola (page 60)
coconut flakes
mixed nuts

Place the milk, yoghurt, honey and vanilla in a bowl and whisk vigorously to ensure everything is well combined. Add the chia seeds and whisk again. Cover with plastic wrap and refrigerate overnight.

In the morning, give the thickened pudding a stir, then serve with your toppings of choice scattered over.

SPICY ALMONDS

MAKES: 155 G (1 CUP)
PREP TIME: 5 MINUTES
COOK TIME: 15 MINUTES

155 g (1 cup) almonds
½ teaspoon smoked paprika
½ teaspoon cayenne pepper
¼ teaspoon salt flakes
¼ teaspoon ground cumin
1 tablespoon olive oil

Preheat the oven to 180°C. Line a baking tray with baking paper.

Combine all the ingredients in a bowl and mix thoroughly.

Spread the almond mixture on the lined tray, then bake in the oven for 15 minutes, or until fragrant and golden brown.

Eat right away or set aside to cool. Store in an airtight container for up to 2 weeks.

To make enough for a crowd, add another cup of your fave nuts to this mixture and double the seasonings.

DATES AND PB

SERVES: 5 (2 DATES EACH)
PREP TIME: 5 MINUTES

10 medjool dates, pitted
3 tablespoons peanut butter

Fill the cavity in each date with a small amount of peanut butter, then spread a layer over the top and eat.

→ *With their super sweet caramel taste, dates are nature's candy. They're great for sweetening up smoothies. These dates taste amazing frozen. Give them a go.*

CRISPY CHICKPEAS

MAKES: 320 G (2 CUPS)
PREP TIME: 5 MINUTES
COOK TIME: 25 MINUTES

2 tablespoons olive oil
320 g (2 cups) canned,
   drained chickpeas
1 teaspoon smoked paprika
1 teaspoon ground cumin
pinch of salt flakes

Preheat the oven to 200°C. Line a baking tray with baking paper.

Heat the olive oil in a small saucepan over medium heat and throw in the chickpeas. Sprinkle over the paprika, cumin and salt and cook, stirring constantly, for 5 minutes, or until heated through.

Tip the spiced chickpeas onto the lined tray and spread out evenly then bake for 20 minutes, or until they are crispy and golden brown.

SEEDY CRACKERS

SERVES: 4
PREP TIME: 10 MINUTES,
PLUS RESTING
COOK TIME: 50 MINUTES

60 g (½ cup) sunflower seeds

70 g (½ cup) pumpkin seeds

40 g (¼ cup) flaxseeds

**40 g (¼ cup) white
    sesame seeds**

2 tablespoons white chia seeds

1 teaspoon salt flakes

**Magic Guacamole (page 128),
    avocado or your choice of
    topping, to serve**

Preheat the oven to 170°C. Line a baking tray with baking paper.

Mix all the ingredients in a bowl, add 250 ml of water and leave to soak for 20–30 minutes until the water is absorbed.

Transfer the mixture to the lined tray and spread out as thinly as possible, then bake for 30 minutes. Remove from the oven and break into bite-sized pieces. Return to the oven to bake for a further 20 minutes, or until crisp and golden.

The crackers are delicious with dip, so serve with Magic Guacamole or your choice of topping.

These are amazing right out of the oven, but can also be stored in an airtight container in the cupboard for up to 2 weeks.

DRESSINGS *and* SAUCES

THE STAPLE DRESSING

VEGAN · GLUTEN-FREE

MAKES: 2–3 TABLESPOONS
PREP TIME: 5 MINUTES

juice of 1 lemon
½ teaspoon dried oregano
pinch each of salt flakes and
**   freshly ground black pepper**
1 tablespoon extra-virgin olive oil

Place all the ingredients in a glass
bowl and whisk well with a fork
until combined.

GARLIC AND CHILLI AIOLI

VEGETARIAN · DAIRY-FREE

MAKES: 140 G
PREP TIME: 5 MINUTES

125 g (½ cup) whole
**   egg mayonnaise**
1 garlic clove, crushed
½ teaspoon chilli flakes
juice of ½ lemon
pinch of salt flakes and freshly
**   ground black pepper**

Place all the ingredients in a glass
bowl and whisk well with a fork
until combined.

LIME AIOLI

VEGETARIAN · DAIRY-FREE

MAKES: 140 G
PREP TIME: 5 MINUTES

zest and juice of ½ lime
125 g (½ cup) whole
**   egg mayonnaise**
1 small garlic clove,
**   crushed**
pinch of salt flakes and
**   freshly ground black**
**   pepper**

Place all the ingredients in a glass
bowl and whisk well with a fork
until combined.

HONEY MUSTARD DRESSING

VEGETARIAN · GLUTEN-FREE
DAIRY-FREE

MAKES: 2 TABLESPOONS
PREP TIME: 5 MINUTES

1 teaspoon honey
½ teaspoon lemon juice
½ teaspoon dijon mustard
3 teaspoons olive oil
pinch of salt flakes

Place all the ingredients in a glass bowl and whisk well with a fork until combined.

MUSTARD SEED DRESSING

VEGAN · GLUTEN-FREE

MAKES: 125 ML (½ CUP)
PREP TIME: 5 MINUTES

2 tablespoons balsamic vinegar
1 tablespoon dijon mustard
125 ml (½ cup) olive oil
1 garlic clove, crushed
½ teaspoon dried oregano
½ teaspoon dried thyme
2 teaspoons wholegrain mustard seeds
pinch of salt flakes and freshly ground black pepper

Place all the ingredients in a glass bowl and whisk well with a fork until combined.

ROCKET AND BASIL PESTO

VEGETARIAN · GLUTEN-FREE

MAKES: 375 G (1½ CUPS)
PREP TIME: 5 MINUTES

100 g (2 cups, tightly packed) basil leaves
70 g (2 cups, tightly packed) rocket leaves
3 tablespoons grated parmesan
60 g (½ cup) slivered almonds
80 g (½ cup) pine nuts
1 tablespoon salt flakes
juice of 1 lemon
170 ml (⅔ cup) light olive oil
2 garlic cloves, crushed

Place all the ingredients in a food processor and process to the desired consistency. I like mine a little chunky.

- 2 WAYS -
VEGGIE CHIPS

CHILLI KALE CHIPS

VEGAN · GLUTEN-FREE

SERVES: 2–3
PREP TIME: 10 MINUTES
COOK TIME: 20 MINUTES

450 g kale, central stems removed

2 tablespoons olive oil

1 teaspoon chilli flakes

1 teaspoon smoked paprika

1 teaspoon salt flakes

pinch of freshly ground black pepper

Preheat the oven to 180°C. Line a baking tray with baking paper.

Tear the kale leaves into pieces the size of your palm or smaller. Place in a large bowl and add the olive oil, chilli flakes, paprika, salt and pepper and mix well.

Spread the seasoned kale on the lined tray and bake for 10 minutes. Remove from the oven, check the chips and, if necessary, return them to the oven for a further 5–10 minutes until super crispy. Eat!

BEETROOT CHIPS

VEGAN

SERVES: 2
PREP TIME: 10 MINUTES
COOK TIME: 20 MINUTES

3 large beetroot, peeled

2 tablespoons olive oil

1 teaspoon salt flakes

2 teaspoons spicy Cajun seasoning

Preheat the oven to 200°C. Line a baking tray with baking paper.

Using a mandoline, cut the beetroot into super-thin slices. If you do not have a mandoline, use a sharp knife to slice them as thinly and evenly as possible. (Getting the slices consistent is important so the chips bake evenly.)

Place the beetroot slices in a bowl and mix in the olive oil, salt and Cajun seasoning.

Arrange the beetroot slices in a single layer on the lined tray and bake in the oven for 20 minutes, or until super crispy.

Mains

SAN CHOY BAU

SERVES: 2–4
PREP TIME: 15 MINUTES
COOK TIME: 20 MINUTES

1 tablespoon sesame oil

2 garlic cloves, crushed

2 cm piece of lemongrass, white part only, very finely sliced

1 long red chilli, finely chopped

10 button mushrooms, cleaned and sliced

2 spring onions, finely sliced

500 g chicken mince

½ teaspoon each of salt flakes and freshly ground black pepper

2 tablespoons soy sauce

3 tablespoons oyster sauce

1 small handful of roughly chopped coriander leaves

6 large iceberg lettuce leaves, trimmed into cups

1 tablespoon lime juice

Heat the sesame oil in a large frying pan over high heat. Add the garlic, lemongrass and chilli and cook, stirring, for 2 minutes, or until fragrant. Stir in the mushrooms and spring onion and cook for 5 minutes.

Add the mince to the pan, season with the salt and pepper and cook, stirring to break up any lumps, until browned and all excess liquid has evaporated, about 7–10 minutes. Stir in the soy and oyster sauces and half the coriander and cook for a further 3 minutes, or until the chicken is cooked through.

Spoon the chicken mixture into the iceberg lettuce cups, top with a squeeze of lime juice and scatter on the remaining coriander.

If you're coeliac – replace the soy sauce with tamari.

GLUTEN-FREE · DAIRY-FREE

CHARGRILLED CHICKEN
with AVOCADO SALSA

SERVES: 2
PREP TIME: 15 MINUTES,
PLUS 1 HOUR MARINATING
COOK TIME: 10 MINUTES

2 chicken breast fillets, trimmed of excess fat

MARINADE
3 garlic cloves, crushed
1 teaspoon each of salt flakes and freshly ground black pepper
1 tablespoon dried oregano
juice of 1 lemon
3 tablespoons olive oil, plus extra for brushing

AVOCADO SALSA
3 tomatoes, diced
1 Lebanese cucumber, diced
1 avocado, diced
1 red onion, finely diced
4 chive stalks, finely chopped
salt flakes and freshly ground black pepper, to taste
juice of ½ lemon

Preheat the oven to 180°C.

To make the marinade, combine the garlic, salt and pepper, dried oregano, lemon juice and olive oil in a large bowl and mix well.

Add the chicken to the marinade and mix to coat thoroughly. Cover and marinate for up to an hour in the fridge.

To make the salsa, place the tomato, cucumber, avocado, onion and chives in a bowl. Sprinkle with salt and pepper, squeeze over the lemon juice and mix thoroughly.

Brush a chargrill pan with a splash of olive oil and place over medium–high heat. Add the chicken and cook for 4 minutes on each side, or until the chicken is charred in patches and cooked through.

Pair your yummy chicken with the salsa and be prepared for your taste buds to go wild.

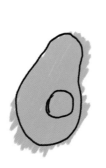

GINGER CHICKEN MEATBALLS
with THAI SALAD

SERVES: 3 • PREP TIME: 15 MINUTES
COOK TIME: 20 MINUTES

olive oil, for frying
1 red capsicum, finely sliced
2 Lebanese cucumbers,
   deseeded and finely sliced
1 red onion, finely sliced
115 g (1½ cups) shredded
   red cabbage
1 large carrot, cut into long,
   thin strips
1 large handful of roughly
   chopped coriander
   leaves (optional)
1 large handful of roughly
   chopped mint

MEATBALLS
500 g chicken mince
2 garlic cloves, crushed
2 cm piece of ginger, grated
1 tablespoon curry powder
2 spring onions, finely sliced
2 tablespoons finely
   chopped coriander leaves
1 tablespoon finely chopped
   mint leaves
pinch of salt flakes
   and freshly ground
   black pepper

DRESSING
1 tablespoon soy sauce
1 small red chilli, deseeded
   and sliced
1 tablespoon sesame oil
2 tablespoons lime juice
1 tablespoon fish sauce
½ teaspoon brown sugar

To make the meatballs, combine the chicken mince, garlic, ginger, curry powder, spring onion, coriander, mint and salt and pepper in a large bowl and mix thoroughly. Using 1 tablespoon of mixture for each ball, roll into bite-sized balls.

Heat a splash of olive oil in a large non-stick frying pan over medium heat, add the meatballs in batches of 8–10 and cook for 5–7 minutes until each and every ball is cooked all the way through.

Place the capsicum, cucumber, onion, cabbage, carrot, coriander (if using) and mint in a large serving bowl and mix.

To make the dressing, in a small bowl, combine the soy sauce, chilli, sesame oil, lime juice, fish sauce and brown sugar and mix thoroughly.

Pour the dressing over the salad and toss. Evenly divide the salad and meatballs between serving plates and serve.

CHICKEN YIROS

SERVES: 4
PREP TIME: 20 MINUTES, PLUS
AT LEAST 1 HOUR TO SET
COOK TIME: 25 MINUTES

500 g chicken breast fillets,
    cut into thin strips
1 teaspoon each of salt
    flakes and freshly ground
    black pepper
1 teaspoon dried oregano
2 garlic cloves, crushed
olive oil, for frying and brushing
4 pita breads
2 tablespoons Greek seasoning
1 onion, finely sliced
3 tomatoes, finely sliced
½ iceberg lettuce, shredded

TZATZIKI

1 kg (4 cups) Greek yoghurt
2–3 Lebanese cucumbers
1 tablespoon olive oil
2–3 garlic cloves, crushed
salt flakes and freshly ground
    black pepper

To make the tzatziki, line a sieve with a Chux cloth and place over a bowl. Spoon the yoghurt into the sieve and leave for 1–2 hours, or best of all overnight, in the fridge. (The longer you leave the yoghurt to strain the thicker it will be.) Tip the strained yoghurt into a bowl. Grate the cucumber into another Chux cloth and squeeze out as much liquid as possible. Add the cucumber, olive oil, garlic and salt and pepper to the yoghurt and mix well. Taste and add more salt to your liking.

Place the chicken strips in a bowl, season with the salt and pepper, add the oregano and garlic and toss.

Heat a splash of olive oil in a large non-stick frying pan over medium–high heat, add the chicken in small batches and cook for 6–8 minutes until the chicken is lightly browned and cooked through.

While the chicken is cooking, brush a little olive oil over the pita bread rounds and sprinkle the Greek seasoning on both sides.

Heat another non-stick frying pan over medium heat and cook the pita rounds on each side for 1 minute.

Spread a generous amount of tzatziki on each warmed pita round. Top with the chicken, onion, tomato and lettuce. Roll up, wrap the base in some baking paper or foil and eat.

→ *This makes a massive amount of tzatziki and is perfect for big parties. It will store in a cling-wrapped bowl in the fridge for up to 1 ½ weeks.*

MEDITERRANEAN STUFFED CHICKEN

SERVES: 3
PREP TIME: 10 MINUTES
COOK TIME: 20 MINUTES

3 chicken breast fillets
2 tablespoons Rocket and
    Basil Pesto (page 139)
75 g (½ cup) sun-dried
    tomatoes, halved
45 g (1 cup) baby spinach leaves
2 slices of mozzarella
6 marinated artichoke hearts,
    drained and quartered
1 garlic clove, crushed
1 tablespoon olive oil
½ teaspoon each of salt
    flakes and freshly ground
    black pepper
½ teaspoon dried oregano
½ teaspoon chilli flakes

Preheat the oven to 180°C. Line a baking tray with baking paper.

Cut a pocket in the middle of each chicken breast, making sure you don't cut all the way through.

Spoon 1 tablespoon of pesto into the pocket of each chicken fillet. Then stuff with the sun-dried tomatoes, baby spinach, mozzarella and artichoke hearts and secure with a toothpick.

Combine the garlic, olive oil, salt and pepper, dried oregano and chilli flakes in a shallow bowl and mix well. Add the stuffed chicken breasts and coat thoroughly.

Heat a large frying pan over high heat, add the chicken and pan-fry for 2 minutes on each side to brown. Transfer to the lined tray and roast in the oven for a further 15 minutes, or until cooked through. Rest for 5 minutes before serving.

LOADED SWEET POTATO SKINS

SERVES: 4
PREP TIME: 10 MINUTES
COOK TIME: 1 HOUR

50 g (¼ cup) quinoa, rinsed
2 sweet potatoes
olive oil, for drizzling
100 g roasted chicken, shredded
5 semi-dried tomatoes,
  cut into strips
2 spring onions, finely chopped
10 pitted kalamata
  olives, halved
salt flakes and freshly ground
  black pepper, to taste
45 g feta, crumbled

Preheat the oven to 200°C. Line a baking tray with baking paper.

Cook the quinoa according to the packet instructions.

Using a fork, pierce the sweet potatoes all over and place on the lined tray. Drizzle on a small amount of olive oil and roast in the oven for 1 hour, or until you can insert a skewer into the centre of each sweet potato with ease.

Cut each sweet potato in half lengthways and scoop out the flesh, leaving a thin layer around the edge.

Place the sweet potato flesh in a bowl, mash and mix in the quinoa, chicken, semi-dried tomatoes, spring onion, olives and salt and pepper. Spoon this mixture back into the sweet potato skins and top with the feta. Eat while still warm.

GREEN CHICKEN CURRY

SERVES: 4
PREP TIME: 15 MINUTES
COOK TIME: 40 MINUTES

2 chicken breast fillets, chopped
   into bite-sized pieces
salt flakes and freshly ground
   black pepper
olive oil, for frying
3–5 long green
   chillies, deseeded
1 cm piece of ginger,
   roughly chopped
2 teaspoons ground coriander
3 tablespoons coriander leaves
2 garlic cloves, crushed
2 tablespoons finely sliced
   spring onion
1 lemongrass stalk, white
   part only, roughly chopped
600 ml coconut cream
4 kaffir lime leaves
2 tablespoons fish sauce
juice of 1 lime
1 handful of basil leaves
125 g (1 cup) topped and tailed
   chopped green beans
60 g (1 cup) broccoli florets
370 g (2 cups) cooked
   basmati rice

Season the chicken with salt and pepper.

Heat a splash of olive oil in a frying pan over medium–high heat, add the chicken in batches and pan-fry on all sides until just golden brown. Set aside for later.

Combine the chilli, ginger, ground coriander and coriander leaves, garlic, spring onion, lemongrass and 1 teaspoon of pepper in a food processor and process to a paste.

Heat 2 tablespoons of olive oil in a saucepan over medium–high heat, add the paste and fry, stirring occasionally, for 3–4 minutes until sizzling and fragrant. Add the chicken, coconut cream and kaffir lime leaves, stir and bring to a simmer, about 3 minutes. Stir in the fish sauce, lime juice and basil and simmer for 20 minutes.

Add the beans and broccoli to the chicken curry and simmer for a few minutes more, or until the vegetables are cooked to your liking. Remove the kaffir lime leaves and serve hot over the cooked rice.

FISH CAKES

MAKES: 10
PREP TIME: 10 MINUTES
COOK TIME: 15 MINUTES

1 tablespoon fish sauce

juice of ½ lime

500 g firm white fish
   fillets (such as ling or
   flathead), pin-boned and
   roughly chopped

2 garlic cloves, crushed

1 large handful of
   coriander leaves

1 egg

3 teaspoons red curry paste

2 spring onions, finely chopped

½ teaspoon salt flakes

3 tablespoons peanut oil

herby Thai salad or sweet chilli
   dipping sauce, to serve

Place the fish sauce, lime juice, fish fillets, garlic, coriander and egg in a food processor and process until combined. Add the curry paste and whiz until mixed through.

Transfer the fish mixture to a bowl. Add the spring onion and salt and mix well. Shape into ten small patties.

Heat the peanut oil in a frying pan over medium heat, add the fish cakes in batches and fry for 2 minutes on each side, or until lightly browned.

Serve your fish cakes with a yummy salad or dipping sauce.

HOMEMADE CHICKEN STOCK

MAKES: ABOUT 2.5 LITRES
(10 CUPS)
PREP TIME: 10 MINUTES
COOK TIME: 3–5 HOURS

1 × 1 kg chicken

1 large onion, quartered

2 carrots, washed

2 potatoes, washed

1 bunch of celery, cut into 10 cm
    lengths (use the leaves)

7 vegetable stock cubes

1 teaspoon each of salt
    flakes and freshly ground
    black pepper

juice of 1 lemon

Place the chicken in a stockpot or very large saucepan (the bigger, the better). Add all the vegetables and cover with about 3 litres of water. Season with the stock cubes and salt and pepper and place over high heat. Bring to the boil, turn the heat to low and simmer for 3–5 hours. Stir in the lemon juice and remove from the heat.

Strain the stock into a large saucepan and use at once or store in airtight containers in the fridge for 3–4 days or freeze for up to 4 weeks.

This nourishing chicken stock can be used for so many things: soups, pasta sauces, broths or as a base for amazing roasts.

SPICED RICE

MAKES: 3 CUPS
PREP TIME: 5 MINUTES
COOK TIME: 20 MINUTES

2 tablespoons butter
1 onion, diced
4 whole cloves
3 whole allspice
200 g (1 cup) basmati rice
375 ml (1½ cups) chicken stock

Melt the butter in a saucepan over high heat, add the onion, cloves and allspice and stir for 3 minutes.

Place the rice in a sieve and rinse under cold water to wash off the excess starch. (This is important: it prevents clumping and gives a cleaner taste.) Add the rice to the pan and cook, stirring to ensure the rice is coated in the onion mixture, for 1 minute. Add the stock and bring to the boil. Immediately reduce the heat to low, cover with the lid and set a timer for 15 minutes. When the timer goes off, you'll have some delicious rice waiting for you.

See opposite for my amazing homemade chicken stock.

DIY BROWN RICE NORI ROLLS

SERVES: 6
PREP TIME: 15 MINUTES,
PLUS 1 HOUR TO SET
COOK TIME: 20 MINUTES

440 g (2 cups) short-grain
  brown rice, rinsed thoroughly
  to remove excess starch
1 tablespoon rice wine vinegar
½ teaspoon salt flakes
6 nori sheets
2 tablespoons
  Japanese mayonnaise
200 g smoked salmon or
  2 × 95 g cans chilli tuna
1 avocado, sliced and/or
  1 carrot, cut into matchsticks

You'll need a sushi mat for this recipe.

Bring 1 litre (4 cups) of water to the boil in a large saucepan. Add the rice and reduce the heat to low. Cover with the lid and cook for 20 minutes, or until the rice is sticky and cooked through. Drain any excess water, add the vinegar and salt and stir through. Set aside.

Grab your sushi mat and place a sheet of nori, shiny side down, on top.

Dip your hands in water (this stops the rice from sticking), grab a handful of the rice, spread over the bottom half of the nori sheet and pat down to form a very thin layer, leaving about a 5mm border from the edge.

Using a fork, make a line down the middle of the rice for your filling. Add a dollop of Japanese mayonnaise and spread this out.

Next up, assemble your filling: add the desired protein (smoked salmon or chilli tuna), avocado and/or carrot. Using the sushi mat, start to roll the nori around the filling as tightly as possible. Pull the mat out and continue to roll to the end. Dampen your fingers with a little water and run along the seam to seal the edge. Repeat until all your nori, rice and fillings have been used. Place in the fridge for an hour to set.

Using a sharp knife, cut each nori roll into four pieces and eat right away.

Nori is Japanese for edible seaweed. Don't let that deter you, though, it's super delicious and nutritious and is a chief ingredient in sushi.

The best thing about sushi is you can include only your faves (mine are smoked salmon and avocado) or whatever you like.

PRAWN *and* VEGGIE PAD THAI

SERVES: 4
PREP TIME: 15 MINUTES
COOK TIME: 15 MINUTES

3 teaspoons soy sauce

2 tablespoons fish sauce

2 tablespoons peanut oil

2 tablespoons tomato paste

1 teaspoon grated ginger

1 mild long red chilli, deseeded
    and finely chopped

2 garlic cloves, crushed

1 head of broccoli,
    cut into florets

100 g (1 cup) topped and
    tailed snow peas

200 g bean sprouts

200 g raw medium prawns,
    shelled and deveined with
    tails intact

4 spring onions, finely sliced,
    plus extra to serve

2 eggs, whisked

250 g dried rice stick noodles,
    cooked according to
    packet instructions

1 handful of roughly chopped
    coriander leaves

90 g (⅓ cup) crushed
    roasted peanuts

Combine the soy and fish sauces, 1 tablespoon of the peanut oil and the tomato paste in a small bowl and stir. Set aside.

Heat the remaining peanut oil in a wok or large saucepan over medium–high heat and add the ginger, chilli and garlic and stir-fry for 1 minute.

Add the broccoli, snow peas and bean sprouts to the wok or pan and stir-fry for 5 minutes. Stir in the prawns and spring onion and cook until the prawns just change colour, about 2 minutes.

Tip the eggs into the work or pan and stir. Add the noodles and sauce mixture and stir-fry for 3 minutes, or until fragrant. Sprinkle on the coriander and toss. Serve with the extra spring onion and the peanuts scattered over the top.

- 4 WAYS -
SALMON
SKEWERS

Pesto (page 168)

Sesame (page 169)

Thai (page 169)

Rosemary (page 168)

- 4 WAYS -
SALMON SKEWERS

PESTO

GLUTEN-FREE · DAIRY-FREE

SERVES: 4-6
PREP TIME: 15 MINUTES
COOK TIME: 6-8 MINUTES

100 g (2 cups, tightly packed) basil leaves,
  plus extra for threading
50 g (⅓ cup) pine nuts, toasted
125 ml (½ cup) extra-virgin olive oil
3 garlic cloves, peeled
pinch of salt flakes and freshly
  ground black pepper
1 tablespoon lemon juice
1 kg salmon fillets, skin removed,
  cut into 2 cm cubes

Soak 10 bamboo skewers in water for at least
an hour.

Combine the basil, pine nuts, olive oil, garlic, salt
and pepper and lemon juice in a food processor
and process to a chunky paste.

Place the salmon in a bowl, add the pesto and toss
to coat. Thread two pieces of salmon onto a skewer,
then add a basil leaf. Repeat until the skewer is full.
Continue with the remaining skewers, salmon and
basil leaves.

Heat the barbecue to hot, add the salmon skewers
and cook on all sides for 6–8 minutes until the fish
is cooked just the way you like it.

ROSEMARY

GLUTEN-FREE · DAIRY-FREE

SERVES: 4-6
PREP TIME: 15 MINUTES
COOK TIME: 6-8 MINUTES

1 kg salmon fillets, skin removed,
  cut into 2 cm cubes
1 teaspoon each of salt flakes and
  freshly ground black pepper
2 teaspoons finely chopped
  rosemary leaves
juice of 1 lemon
8 asparagus spears, woody ends
  trimmed, cut into 3 cm lengths

Soak 10 bamboo skewers in water for at least
an hour.

Place the salmon in a large bowl, add the salt and
pepper, rosemary and lemon juice and mix well.

Thread two pieces of salmon onto a skewer, then
add two to three pieces of asparagus. Repeat until
the skewer is full. Continue with the remaining
skewers, salmon and asparagus.

Heat the barbecue to hot, add the salmon skewers
and cook on all sides for 6–8 minutes until the fish
is cooked just the way you like it.

THAI

DAIRY-FREE

SERVES: 4-6
PREP TIME: 15 MINUTES
COOK TIME: 6-8 MINUTES

1 kg salmon fillets, skin removed,
    cut into 2 cm cubes
2 tablespoons sesame oil
3 tablespoons soy sauce
juice of 1 lime
1 tablespoon fish sauce
1 lemongrass stalk, white part only,
    finely sliced
2 garlic cloves, sliced into slivers
2 cm piece of ginger, sliced into slivers
1 spring onion, finely sliced
1 small red chilli, deseeded and finely sliced
2 tablespoons roughly chopped
    coriander leaves
3 limes, sliced into thin wedges

Soak 10 bamboo skewers in water for at least
an hour.

Place the salmon, sesame oil, soy sauce, lime
juice, fish sauce, lemongrass, garlic, ginger, spring
onion, chilli and coriander in a large bowl and mix
thoroughly to ensure the salmon is evenly coated.

Thread two pieces of salmon onto a skewer, then
add a wedge of lime. Repeat until the skewer is full.
Continue with the remaining skewers, salmon and
lime wedges.

Heat the barbecue to hot, add the salmon skewers
and cook on all sides for 6–8 minutes until the fish
is cooked just the way you like it.

SESAME

GLUTEN-FREE · DAIRY-FREE

SERVES: 4-6
PREP TIME: 15 MINUTES
COOK TIME: 6-8 MINUTES

1 kg salmon fillets, skin removed,
    cut into 2 cm cubes
2 tablespoons dried oregano
2 teaspoons sesame seeds
1 teaspoon each of salt flakes and
    freshly ground black pepper
1 teaspoon ground turmeric
1 tablespoon finely chopped
    coriander leaves
¼ teaspoon chilli flakes
2 tablespoons olive oil
20 cherry tomatoes

Soak 10 bamboo skewers in water for at least
an hour.

Place the salmon, oregano, sesame seeds, salt
and pepper, turmeric, coriander, chilli flakes and
olive oil in a bowl and gently toss to coat the
salmon thoroughly.

Thread two pieces of salmon onto a skewer, add
a tomato, then thread on another two pieces of
salmon and another tomato. Repeat until the
skewer is full. Continue with the remaining skewers,
salmon and tomatoes.

Heat the barbecue to hot, add the salmon skewers
and cook on all sides for 6–8 minutes until the fish
is cooked just the way you like it.

*Serve your salmon skewers with
a leafy green salad and some
steamed brown rice.*

SPINACH and ALMOND PESTO SALMON

SERVES: 2
PREP TIME: 10 MINUTES
COOK TIME: 30 MINUTES

1 red capsicum, finely sliced

2 carrots, halved lengthways
   and sliced into thin strips

6 asparagus spears, woody
   ends trimmed

2 handfuls of green beans,
   topped and tailed

1 red onion, cut into wedges

2 garlic cloves, crushed

pinch of salt flakes and freshly
   ground black pepper

olive oil, for drizzling

2 × 150 g salmon fillets, skin on

steamed brown rice or leafy,
   veggie-packed salad, to serve

SPINACH AND ALMOND PESTO

100 g (2 cups, tightly packed)
   basil leaves

70 g (1 ½ cups, tightly packed)
   spinach leaves

3 tablespoons grated parmesan

60 g (½ cup) slivered almonds

80 g (½ cup) pine nuts, toasted

1 tablespoon salt flakes

juice of 1 lemon

170 ml (⅔ cup) light olive oil

2 garlic cloves, crushed

Preheat the oven to 180°C. Line a baking tray with baking paper.

Combine all the pesto ingredients in a food processor and whiz to a paste. I like mine a little chunky but the consistency is up to you.

Place the capsicum, carrot, asparagus, beans and onion on the lined tray. Sprinkle the garlic over the top, season with salt and pepper and drizzle on the olive oil. Roast in the oven for 15 minutes. Remove the tray and place the salmon on the bed of veggies. Return to the oven and bake for a further 15 minutes, or until the salmon is cooked to your liking.

Spoon 1 tablespoon of pesto over each salmon fillet. Divide the salmon and veggies between serving bowls and eat with rice or a salad.

As this pesto recipe makes more than is needed, store the remaining pesto in an airtight container in the fridge for up to a week. It can be used as a pasta sauce, as a topping on toast or as a dip when entertaining.

NASI GORENG

SERVES: 4
PREP TIME: 20 MINUTES
COOK TIME: 25 MINUTES

3 tablespoons peanut oil

1 onion, diced

¼ teaspoon shrimp paste

3 spring onions, finely sliced

2 garlic cloves, crushed

4 cm piece of ginger, grated

2 long red chillies, deseeded
   and finely chopped

100 g shiitake
   mushrooms, cleaned

1 handful of baby corn, chopped

250 g choy sum, roughly
   chopped into 2 cm pieces

555 g (3 cups) cooked
   long-grain brown rice

4 eggs

2 tablespoons kecap manis

juice of ½ lime

3 tablespoons soy sauce

1 large handful of roughly
   chopped coriander leaves

2 tablespoons fried shallots

lime wedges, to serve

Splash the peanut oil into a wok or large saucepan over medium–high heat, add the onion, shrimp paste, spring onion, garlic, ginger and chilli and stir-fry for 3 minutes, or until the onion is softened.

Add the mushrooms, baby corn and choy sum to the wok or pan and stir-fry for 5 minutes. Toss in the cooked rice and stir through.

Meanwhile, poach the eggs and set aside. For how to poach eggs, see page 37.

In a small bowl, mix the kecap manis, lime juice and soy sauce. Pour over the rice mixture and stir thoroughly.

Divide the rice between serving bowls, top with the egg, coriander and fried shallots and serve with the lime wedges.

1 cup uncooked brown rice = 3 cups cooked.

ALMOND MEAL FISH FINGERS

SERVES: 2
PREP TIME: 15 MINUTES
COOK TIME: 10 MINUTES

100 g (1 cup) almond meal
1 tablespoon smoked paprika
1 tablespoon dried oregano
pinch of salt flakes and freshly
    ground black pepper
1 egg
2 × 150 g flathead fillets
    (or any firm white fish),
    skin removed, pin-boned
olive or coconut oil, for frying

TO SERVE
lemon wedges
Spicy Sweet Potato Chips
    (page 98)

Combine the almond meal, paprika, dried oregano and salt and pepper in a shallow bowl.

Whisk the egg in a separate shallow bowl.

Cut the fish into 'fingers', dip in the egg, then coat evenly in the almond meal mix.

Heat the oil in a large frying pan over medium–high heat, add the fish and cook for 3 minutes on each side, or until crispy and golden. Drain on paper towel. Serve with a squeeze of lemon and some sweet potato chips.

PASTA with SLOW-COOKED BEEF RAGU

SERVES: 4–6
PREP TIME: 20 MINUTES
COOK TIME: 4–8 HOURS

1 kg sirloin steak, cut into cubes

1 teaspoon each of salt
   flakes and freshly ground
   black pepper

3 tablespoons olive oil

1 large onion, diced

1 small red chilli, deseeded
   and finely sliced

2 garlic cloves, crushed

2 tablespoons tomato paste

750 ml (3 cups) tomato passata

5 whole allspice

5 whole cloves

5 basil leaves, torn

500 g dried spaghetti

grated parmesan and basil
   leaves, to serve

You'll need a slow cooker for this recipe.

Season the beef with the salt and pepper.

Heat 2 tablespoons of the olive oil in a large saucepan over medium heat, add the meat and cook for 3–4 minutes on all sides until lightly browned. Transfer the meat to your slow cooker.

In the same pan, heat the remaining oil over medium heat and lightly fry the onion, chilli and garlic for 5 minutes, or until the onion is softened.

Transfer the onion mixture to the slow cooker and add the tomato paste, passata, allspice, cloves, basil and 250 ml of water and sprinkle on some extra salt and pepper. Cook for 4 hours on high, or 8 hours on low.

Cook the pasta in boiling salted water until al dente. Drain well.

Serve the deliciously rich and tender meat sauce with the pasta and a sprinkle of parmesan and a scattering of basil leaves.

If you don't have a slow cooker, this ragu can be cooked on the stovetop. Leave to simmer for 1 hour over super-low heat to get that meat super tender.

- 3 WAYS -
TACOS

MUSHROOM

VEGETARIAN

SERVES: 6
PREP TIME: 15 MINUTES
COOK TIME: 15 MINUTES

2 tablespoons olive oil

20 mixed button and Swiss brown mushrooms, cleaned and sliced

2 tablespoons Taco Spice Mix (see opposite)

TO SERVE

6 corn tortillas

¼ iceberg lettuce, shredded

2 avocados, sliced

1 red onion, finely sliced

2 tomatoes, diced

125 g (1 cup) grated tasty cheese (optional)

1 small handful of finely chopped coriander leaves

juice of ½ lime

Heat the olive oil in a large frying pan over medium-high heat, add the mushrooms and cook, stirring occasionally, for 8–10 minutes until all excess liquid has evaporated. Add the spice mix and cook, stirring, for 1 minute.

Heat the tortillas in a microwave for 10 seconds or in a small frying pan for 30 seconds on each side until soft.

Divide the mushroom filling between the tortillas and layer on the lettuce, avocado, onion, tomato and cheese (if using). Scatter over the coriander, squeeze on the lime juice and you're ready to go.

TOFU

VEGETARIAN

SERVES: 6
PREP TIME: 15 MINUTES
COOK TIME: 15 MINUTES

200 g firm tofu, sliced

3 tablespoons Taco Spice Mix (see opposite)

1 tablespoon light olive oil

TO SERVE

6 corn tortillas

¼ iceberg lettuce, shredded

2 avocados, sliced

1 red onion, finely sliced

2 tomatoes, diced

125 g (1 cup) grated tasty cheese (optional)

1 small handful of finely chopped coriander leaves

juice of ½ lime

Place the tofu in a bowl, add the spice mix and toss gently to coat. Set aside to marinate for 10 minutes.

Heat the olive oil in a frying pan, add the tofu and fry on all sides for 5–7 minutes until lightly browned.

Heat the tortillas in a microwave for 10 seconds or in a small frying pan for 30 seconds on each side until soft.

Divide the tofu filling between the tortillas and layer on the lettuce, avocado, onion, tomato and cheese (if using). Scatter over the coriander, squeeze on the lime juice and you're ready to go.

BEEF

SERVES: 6
PREP TIME: 15 MINUTES
COOK TIME: 15 MINUTES

2 tablespoons olive oil

1 onion, diced

1 garlic clove, crushed

500 g beef mince

½ teaspoon each of salt flakes and freshly
    ground black pepper

1 × 400 g can kidney beans

1½ tablespoons Taco Spice Mix (see right)

3 coriander stalks with leaves, roughly chopped

100 g (½ cup) diced tomatoes

250 ml (1 cup) tomato passata

125 ml (½ cup) beef stock or water

TO SERVE

6 corn tortillas

¼ iceberg lettuce, shredded

2 avocados, sliced

1 red onion, finely sliced

2 tomatoes, diced

125 g (1 cup) grated tasty cheese (optional)

1 small handful of finely chopped coriander

juice of ½ lime

Heat the olive oil in a frying pan over medium heat, add the onion and garlic and cook, stirring occasionally, for 5 minutes, or until the onion is softened. Add the beef, stirring to break up any lumps, season with the salt and pepper and cook for a further 5–7 minutes. Stir in the kidney beans, spice mix and roughly chopped coriander and cook for 5 minutes, continuing to stir. Add the diced tomatoes, passata and stock or water and simmer for 15 minutes, or until the ragu is thick.

Heat the tortillas in a microwave for 10 seconds or in a small frying pan for 30 seconds on each side until soft. **>>**

>> Divide the beef filling between the tortillas and layer on the lettuce, avocado, onion, tomato and cheese (if using). Scatter over the finely chopped coriander, squeeze on the lime juice and you're ready to go.

TACO SPICE MIX

SERVES: 6
PREP TIME: 15 MINUTES

1 tablespoon chilli powder

½ teaspoon garlic powder

¼ teaspoon onion powder

¼ teaspoon dried oregano

½ teaspoon smoked paprika

½ teaspoon ground cumin

1 teaspoon salt flakes

Combine all the spice mix ingredients in a bowl and mix well.

LEMONGRASS BEEF BURRITO BOWLS

SERVES: 4 • PREP TIME: 20 MINUTES, PLUS 1 HOUR MARINATING
COOK TIME: 45 MINUTES

1 long red chilli, deseeded
   and finely sliced
1 lemongrass stalk, white
   part only, finely sliced
2 garlic cloves, crushed
2 cm piece of ginger, grated
juice of ½ lime
2 tablespoons soy sauce
1 tablespoon fish sauce
1 tablespoon sesame oil
500 g beef sirloin, cut
   into strips
300 g (1½ cups) long-grain
   brown rice
2 teaspoons olive oil

200 g canned, drained
   corn kernels
1 handful of shredded
   iceberg lettuce
lime wedges, to serve

BEANS
olive oil, for frying
80 g (½ cup) canned,
   drained black beans
80 g (½ cup) canned,
   drained chickpeas
¼ teaspoon garlic salt
¼ teaspoon cayenne pepper
¼ teaspoon smoked paprika

GUACAMOLE
2 avocados, diced
juice of ½ lemon
salt flakes and freshly
   ground black pepper

SALSA
2 small tomatoes, diced
½ red onion, finely diced
1 tablespoon finely chopped
   coriander leaves,
   plus extra to serve
juice of ½ lime

Combine the chilli, lemongrass, garlic, ginger, lime juice, soy sauce, fish sauce and sesame oil in a food processor and whiz to a smooth paste.

Place the beef in a bowl, add the paste and toss to coat. Cover with plastic wrap and place in the fridge for 1 hour to marinate.

Cook the rice in boiling salted water for 30–35 minutes until tender. Drain well.

To make the beans, heat a small splash of olive oil in a non-stick frying pan over medium–high heat, add the black beans, chickpeas, garlic salt, cayenne pepper and paprika and cook, stirring occasionally, for 5 minutes, or until sizzling and fragrant.

To make the guacamole, mash the avocados in a bowl and add the lemon juice and salt and pepper to taste.

To make the salsa, place the tomato, onion and coriander in a small bowl and mix well. Squeeze on the lime juice and sprinkle over ¼ teaspoon of salt.

Heat the olive oil in a frying pan over medium–high heat, add the beef in small batches (to ensure the strips don't stew) and stir constantly until browned, 5–6 minutes.

Divide the rice, corn, lettuce, beans, beef, salsa and guacamole between serving bowls. Serve with the lime wedges and extra coriander.

BEEF *and* BROWN RICE STIR-FRY

SERVES: 4
PREP TIME: 15 MINUTES
COOK TIME: 30 MINUTES

400 g fillet steak, sliced
    into thin strips
salt flakes and freshly
    ground black pepper
2 teaspoons dried oregano
olive oil, for frying
½ onion, finely diced
1 garlic clove, crushed
1 small red chilli, deseeded
    and finely sliced
1 head of broccoli,
    cut into florets
2 carrots, finely sliced
1 handful of green beans,
    topped and tailed
½ red capsicum, finely sliced
5 button mushrooms,
    cleaned and quartered
1 tablespoon sesame oil
2 tablespoons soy sauce
2 tablespoons oyster sauce
370 g (2 cups) cooked
    long-grain brown rice
2 tablespoons roughly
    chopped coriander leaves

Place the beef in a bowl, sprinkle over some salt
and pepper and the dried oregano and toss to coat.

Heat a splash of olive oil in a wok or large saucepan over
medium–high heat, add the beef in small batches and stir-fry
until the meat is browned, 5–6 minutes. Set aside.

Splash some more olive oil into the hot wok or pan, add
the onion, garlic and chilli and cook for 2 minutes over
medium–high heat. Throw in all the veggies and stir-fry
for 10 minutes, or until cooked to your liking.

Meanwhile, in a small bowl, mix together the sesame oil,
soy sauce and oyster sauce.

Return the beef to the wok, add the rice and pour on
the dressing, stirring to ensure the rice is evenly coated.
Divide between serving bowls and serve with the coriander
scattered over the top.

PULLED PORK SLIDERS

MAKES: 12
PREP TIME: 30 MINUTES
COOK TIME: 4–8 HOURS

1 tablespoon olive oil
1 × 2 kg pork shoulder,
    trimmed of fat
2 onions, finely sliced
250 ml (1 cup) apple juice
12 slider buns

DRY RUB

2 large garlic cloves, crushed
1 tablespoon salt flakes
2 tablespoons fennel seeds
1 tablespoon black peppercorns
2 tablespoons chilli flakes
1 teaspoon cumin seeds
1 teaspoon coriander seeds
1 teaspoon ground turmeric
1 tablespoon smoked paprika

SAUCE

2 tablespoons dijon mustard
125 ml (½ cup) tomato passata
freshly ground black pepper
1 tablespoon apple
    cider vinegar

SALAD

¼ red cabbage, shredded
2 green apples, finely sliced
20 g (⅓ cup) chopped mint
20 g (⅓ cup) chopped
    coriander leaves
2 spring onions, finely sliced
juice of ½ lemon

You'll need a slow cooker for this recipe.

To make the dry rub, using a blender or mortar and pestle, grind the garlic and all the spices to a fine paste.

Heat the olive oil in a large frying pan over medium–high heat. Add the pork and brown for 2 minutes on each side. Transfer to a chopping board and, with a sharp pointed knife, poke small pockets randomly into the pork flesh, then rub the dry spice mix into the cuts and over the pork to cover completely.

Place the onion and a sprinkle of salt in your slow cooker. Add the pork and apple juice and cook on high for 4 hours, or low for 8 hours. Remove the pork and shred into small pieces with two forks.

Place all the sauce ingredients in a saucepan and bring to the boil. Add the shredded pork and mix well.

Combine the salad ingredients in a large serving bowl and toss gently.

Slice the buns in half, fill with the pork and salad and serve.

If you don't have a slow cooker, you can use your oven. Place the spice-rubbed pork in a large roasting tin, pour in 250 ml (1 cup) of water – in addition to the apple juice – cover with foil and roast at 150°C for 3–4 hours.

MEDITERRANEAN MEATBALL SKEWERS

MAKES: 8
PREP TIME: 20 MINUTES
COOK TIME: 20–30 MINUTES

500 g lean beef mince

1 egg

1 onion, grated

2 garlic cloves, crushed

3 tablespoons finely chopped
flat-leaf parsley

1 tablespoon finely
chopped mint

½ teaspoon ground cumin

½ teaspoon salt flakes

1 teaspoon freshly ground
black pepper

25 g (¼ cup) grated parmesan

½ red capsicum, cut into
2 cm squares

½ yellow capsicum, cut into
2 cm squares

½ green capsicum, cut into
2 cm squares

Tzatziki (page 150), to serve

Soak 8 bamboo skewers in water for 1 hour.

Preheat the oven to 180°C. Line a baking tray with
baking paper.

Combine the beef, egg, onion, garlic, parsley, mint, cumin,
salt, pepper and parmesan in a large bowl and mix well
with your hands. Shape into bite-sized balls and thread
onto the skewers, alternating with the different coloured
capsicum pieces.

Place the skewers on the lined tray and bake in the oven
for 20 minutes, or until the meatballs are cooked through.
Be careful not to overcook them as they can dry out.

These skewers are delicious served with tzatziki as
a dipping sauce.

LAMB
SKEWERS

The Classic (page 188)

Oyster and soy (page 188)

Chimichurri (page 189)

- 3 WAYS -
LAMB SKEWERS

THE CLASSIC

GLUTEN-FREE · DAIRY-FREE

MAKES: 10 SKEWERS
PREP TIME: 15 MINUTES
PLUS 1 HOUR MARINATING
COOK TIME: 10-15 MINUTES

500 g lamb shoulder, cut into 3 cm cubes

2 garlic cloves, crushed

2 tablespoons dried oregano

1½ tablespoons salt flakes

1 tablespoon freshly ground black pepper

3 tablespoons olive oil

1 red capsicum, cut into 2 cm squares

1 large red onion, cut into 2 cm pieces

1 zucchini, cut into rounds

Soak 10 bamboo skewers in water for 1 hour.

Place the lamb in a bowl, add the garlic, oregano, salt, pepper and olive oil and mix well. Cover with plastic wrap and marinate in the fridge for 1 hour.

Thread the lamb cubes onto the skewers, alternating with the capsicum, onion and zucchini.

Heat your barbecue to hot, add the skewers and cook for 6–10 minutes on all sides, until they are cooked to your liking.

OYSTER AND SOY

DAIRY-FREE

MAKES: 10 SKEWERS
PREP TIME: 15 MINUTES
PLUS 1 HOUR MARINATING
COOK TIME: 10 MINUTES

500 g lamb shoulder, cut into 2 cm cubes

2 garlic cloves, crushed

1 small red chilli, deseeded and finely chopped

1 tablespoon finely chopped flat-leaf parsley

2 tablespoons oyster sauce

2 tablespoons soy sauce

2 tablespoons olive oil

juice of 1 lemon

Soak 10 bamboo skewers in water for 1 hour.

Place the lamb in a bowl, add the garlic, chilli, parsley, oyster and soy sauces, olive oil and lemon juice and mix well. Cover with plastic wrap and marinate in the fridge for 1 hour.

Thread the lamb cubes onto the skewers.

Heat your barbecue to hot, add the skewers and cook for 6–10 minutes on all sides, until the lamb is cooked to your liking.

CHIMICHURRI

GLUTEN-FREE · DAIRY-FREE

MAKES: 10 SKEWERS
PREP TIME: 15 MINUTES
PLUS 1 HOUR MARINATING
COOK TIME: 10-15 MINUTES

20 g (1 cup, tightly packed) flat-leaf
   parsley leaves
15 g (½ cup, tightly packed) coriander leaves
1 spring onion, roughly chopped
1 jalapeno chilli, deseeded
5 garlic cloves, roasted (nicer taste but you
   can use fresh)
1 teaspoon chilli flakes
½ teaspoon smoked paprika
salt flakes and freshly ground black pepper
125 ml (½ cup) olive oil
125 ml (½ cup) lime juice (about 4 limes)
500 g lamb shoulder, cut into 2 cm cubes
leafy green salad and/or roasted potatoes,
   to serve

Soak 10 bamboo skewers in water for 1 hour.

Place the parsley, coriander, spring onion, jalapeno, garlic, chilli flakes, paprika, 1 teaspoon of salt and ¼ teaspoon of pepper in a food processor and pulse. While blending, slowly drizzle in the olive oil and lime juice and process to a thick green sauce. Taste and adjust seasoning accordingly.

Sprinkle a little salt and pepper over the lamb, then thread the cubes onto the skewers.

Heat your barbecue to hot, add the skewers and cook for 6–10 minutes on all sides, until cooked to your liking.

Top your lamb skewers with the chimichurri sauce and pair with a salad and/or potatoes.

— HOW TO —
ROAST GARLIC

Preheat the oven to 180°C.

Grab a whole garlic bulb, then chop off the top quarter so you can see the cloves. Sprinkle on 1 tablespoon of olive oil and a little salt and wrap tightly in foil. Roast for 30 minutes, or until the garlic cloves are very soft when pierced with a skewer. Refrigerate for 2 weeks or freeze for 2 months.

What you can use it for:

♥ spread on biscuits (check out my Seedy Crackers on page 136)

♥ add to salad dressings

♥ mash into dips to give them a smoky flavour

♥ use in place of raw garlic in sauces.

BURST TOMATO and LAMB SALAD

SERVES: 2
PREP TIME: 10 MINUTES
COOK TIME: 15 MINUTES

250 g cherry tomatoes

2 tablespoons olive oil

salt flakes and freshly
    ground black pepper

1 × 200 g lamb backstrap

2 garlic cloves, crushed

1 rosemary sprig, leaves picked

1 Lebanese cucumber,
    finely sliced

135 g (3 cups) baby
    spinach leaves

½ red onion, finely sliced
    into rings

5 mint leaves, roughly chopped

1 small handful of roughly
    chopped coriander leaves

1 tablespoon lemon juice

Preheat the oven to 200°C. Line a baking tray with baking paper.

Coat the cherry tomatoes in 1 tablespoon of the olive oil and sprinkle with salt and pepper. Tip onto the lined tray and roast in the oven for 10–15 minutes until the tomatoes are bursting from their skins. Set aside to cool.

Place the lamb in a shallow bowl and add the garlic, rosemary, ¼ teaspoon each of salt and pepper and the remaining olive oil.

Place a chargrill pan over high heat, add the lamb and cook to your liking, 3–4 minutes on each side for slightly pink in the middle, a minute or two longer for well done. Set aside to rest in a warm place for 5 minutes.

Combine the cucumber, spinach, onion, mint, coriander and tomatoes in a bowl and mix well.

Using a sharp knife, slice the lamb into thin strips and add to the salad. Drizzle on the lemon juice, sprinkle on a little salt and pepper and toss gently.

STUFFED STEAK

SERVES: 4
PREP TIME: 20 MINUTES
COOK TIME: 45 MINUTES

**750 g skirt steak, cut into
   eight long, thin strips**
2 garlic cloves, crushed
**salt flakes and freshly ground
   black pepper**
3 tablespoons olive oil
1 red onion, diced
**15 button mushrooms,
   cleaned and sliced**
**150 g (1 cup) halved
   semi-dried tomatoes**
1 handful of baby spinach leaves
**8 slices of mozzarella
   or provolone**
**500 g (2 cups) Classic
   Napoletana Sauce
   (page 207)**

Preheat the oven to 200°C.

Place a piece of baking paper on top of each steak, then pound with a mallet (or rolling pin) to about 5 mm thick.

Sprinkle the garlic over the steaks and season with a little salt and pepper. Set aside.

Heat 1 tablespoon of the olive oil in a small frying pan over high heat, add the onion and mushrooms and fry for 5–8 minutes until the onion is softened.

Cover each piece of steak with a thin layer of the mushroom mixture, add 2–3 semi-dried tomatoes, 3–4 spinach leaves and a slice of cheese. Tightly roll up, ensuring you keep the filling inside, and secure with 2–3 toothpicks.

Heat the remaining olive oil in a large frying pan over medium-high heat, add the involtini and cook until lightly browned, about 2 minutes on each side.

Transfer the involtini to a baking dish and top with the napoletana sauce. Bake in the oven for 20–30 minutes until the meat is tender.

Be sure to remove all the toothpicks before eating.

PERFECT ROAST PORK

SERVES: 6
PREP TIME: 15 MINUTES
COOK TIME: 3 HOURS

1 × 2 kg boneless pork
  shoulder, trimmed of fat
4 garlic cloves, sliced into
  thin slivers
2 tablespoons salt flakes
1 tablespoon freshly ground
  black pepper
3 rosemary sprigs,
  roughly chopped
2 tablespoons dried oregano
375 ml (1½ cups) vegetable
  stock, plus extra if needed
3 potatoes, cut into 4 cm cubes
3 carrots, halved lengthways
12 button mushrooms, cleaned
juice of 1 lemon
salad, to serve

Preheat the oven to 180°C.

Using a sharp knife, score the pork all over in a crisscross pattern, then randomly pierce the flesh all over with the tip of the knife to make deep pockets. Place the garlic slivers in these small pockets to ensure the meat is getting that extra bit of flavour.

Combine the salt, pepper, rosemary and oregano in a small bowl, then rub over the pork.

Transfer the pork to a large baking dish, pour on the vegetable stock, cover with a lid or some foil and place in the oven for 2 hours. Remove from the oven. If the pork looks a little dry, pour some extra vegetable stock on top. Throw in the veggies, drizzle lemon juice over the veggies then return to the oven and roast for 1 hour, or until the pork is very tender and the vegetables are soft. Leave to sit for 5 minutes before slicing.

Slice the pork into thin strips. Serve the pork and veggies paired with some yummy salad.

This recipe can also be used for beef and lamb.

THE
Veggie
-PATCH-

FETTUCCINE PUTTANESCA

SERVES: 4-6
PREP TIME: 15 MINUTES
COOK TIME: 20 MINUTES

400 g fettuccine or Fresh
   Chilli and Basil Fettuccine
   (page 202)
olive oil, for cooking, plus
   a little extra
½ onion, diced
2 garlic cloves, crushed
1 small red chilli, deseeded
   and finely chopped
3 tablespoons finely chopped
   flat-leaf parsley
5 finely chopped basil leaves
3 tablespoons baby capers
80 g (½ cup) pitted and halved
   kalamata olives
220 g (1½ cups) halved
   cherry tomatoes
salt flakes and freshly ground
   black pepper
shaved parmesan, to serve

Cook the fettuccine in boiling salted water until al dente. Drain well.

Meanwhile, heat the olive oil in a saucepan over medium heat. Add the onion, garlic, chilli, parsley and basil and cook, stirring occasionally, for 5 minutes, or until the onion is translucent. Stir in the capers and olives and cook for 3 minutes.

Add the cherry tomatoes to the pan and cook for 5 minutes, or until the tomatoes are softened and starting to burst. Add a touch more olive oil and throw in the drained pasta. Taste and season with salt and pepper. Transfer to serving bowls and top with a generous scattering of parmesan.

VEGGIE PASTA SAUCE

SERVES: 6–8
PREP TIME: 20 MINUTES
COOK TIME: 55 MINUTES

1 head of cauliflower,
    cut into florets
1 carrot, trimmed
2 zucchini, trimmed
10 button mushrooms, cleaned
1 large onion, quartered
3 tablespoons olive oil
3 garlic cloves, crushed
2 tablespoons tomato paste
3 × 400 g cans whole peeled
    tomatoes, crushed
1 teaspoon dried oregano
1 teaspoon each of salt
    flakes and freshly
    ground black pepper
1 small red chilli, deseeded
    and chopped
5 basil leaves, roughly torn
cooked spaghetti, to serve

Using a food processor, and working with one vegetable at a time, process the cauliflower, carrot, zucchini, mushrooms and onion until finely chopped. As each vegetable is processed, combine in a bowl.

Heat the olive oil in a large saucepan over high heat, throw in all the chopped vegetables and cook, stirring, for 10 minutes. Add the garlic and cook, stirring now and then, for 15 minutes, or until the vegetables are very soft. Stir in the tomato paste, crushed tomatoes, oregano and salt and pepper and simmer for 20 minutes.

Add the chilli and basil to the pan and simmer for a further 10 minutes, or until the sauce is reduced and thick. Taste; if the sauce needs more seasoning, add to your liking.

Serve with some yummy spaghetti or spoon into airtight containers and store in the fridge for up to 5 days or freeze for up to 3 months.

The reason we process the veggies separately is to avoid a mushy paste; rather, we want yummy chunky vegetables.

FRESH CHILLI *and* BASIL FETTUCCINE

SERVES: 4
PREP TIME: 1 HOUR
COOK TIME: 5 MINUTES

300 g (2 cups) plain flour,
   sifted, plus extra for dusting
½ teaspoon salt flakes
½ teaspoon chilli flakes
2 tablespoons dried basil
¼ teaspoon freshly ground
   black pepper
5 eggs, whisked

You'll need a pasta machine for this recipe.

Combine the flour, salt, chilli flakes, dried basil and pepper in a bowl and mix thoroughly.

Create a well in the flour mixture, add the eggs and whisk, gradually drawing in the flour from the outside of the bowl, until a very soft dough forms.

Lightly dust your clean kitchen benchtop with some extra flour and turn out the dough. Gently knead, folding the dough over and over until it starts to firm up, around 5 minutes. Sprinkle on more flour as needed so the dough doesn't stick to your benchtop.

Cut the dough in half with a sharp knife, if you see lots of air bubbles, keep kneading. The dough is perfect when it forms a smooth elastic ball with only a few air bubbles when cut.

Sprinkle more flour over the benchtop and divide the dough into four equal portions. Sprinkle each portion with flour.

Set your pasta machine to the thickest setting. Flatten a portion of dough and feed through the machine twice. Fold into thirds (it will look like a letter in the mail) and feed through a couple more times.

Dust the dough sheet with a little flour and run it through progressively thinner settings on the machine, rolling it through each setting two or three times (don't skip any settings, this process takes time). If the pasta sheet gets too long and you don't have an extra set of hands, place on a chopping board and cut in half. Continue to roll the pasta sheet through until about 1 mm thick – or as thin as you'd like it to be.

To make the fettuccine, switch the setting from pasta roller to cutter and run the pasta sheet through the cutter. >>

Recipe continues on page 204.

Recipe continued from page 202.

>> Toss the fettuccine in a little flour to prevent sticking, then place on a tray. Repeat these steps with the remaining portions of dough.

Bring a large saucepan of salted water to the boil. Add the fettuccine and cook until al dente, about 5 minutes. Drain and toss in some delicious sauce.

The fettuccine, covered with plastic wrap or foil, can be stored in the fridge for up to 3 days. To freeze the fettuccine, place in portion-size bundles in an airtight container, cover with a lid and freeze for up to 3 months.

If the pasta begins to break when feeding through the pasta machine, don't give up. Roll it back up into a ball, knead a little more and start over.

CLASSIC NAPOLETANA SAUCE

SERVES: 6-8
PREP TIME: 10 MINUTES
COOK TIME: 35 MINUTES

1 tablespoon olive oil

1 onion, diced

2 garlic cloves, crushed

2 tablespoons tomato paste

2 × 400 g cans whole peeled
   tomatoes, crushed

1 teaspoon dried oregano

1 teaspoon chilli flakes (more
   if you like it extra hot)

1 teaspoon each of salt
   flakes and freshly ground
   black pepper

5 basil leaves, roughly torn

Heat the olive oil in a large saucepan over medium–high heat, add the onion and garlic and fry, stirring now and then, for 5 minutes, or until the onion is softened. Add the tomato paste and stir for 1 minute.

Pour the crushed tomatoes into the pan, add the dried oregano, chilli flakes and salt and pepper, reduce the heat to low and simmer for 15 minutes. Add the basil and simmer for a further 10 minutes, or until the sauce is thick. Serve at once or store in the fridge for up to 3 days or freeze in small containers for up to 3 months.

This is yummy served with fresh pasta – check out my Chilli and Basil Fettuccine (page 202) or Sweet Potato and Basil Gnocchi (page 210) – and a generous sprinkle of freshly grated parmesan.

STUFFED VEGETABLES
with QUINOA

SERVES: 4
PREP TIME: 45 MINUTES
COOK TIME: 1 HOUR,
40 MINUTES

4 tomatoes

2 zucchini

1 eggplant

2 red capsicums

3 tablespoons olive oil

1 onion, finely diced

2 garlic cloves, crushed

1 long red chilli

1 large handful of finely
   chopped flat-leaf parsley

1 handful of chopped mint

125 ml (½ cup) tomato passata

3 tablespoons tomato paste

salt flakes and freshly ground
   black pepper

185 g quinoa, rinsed

salad or veggies, to serve

Preheat the oven to 180°C. Line a large baking dish with baking paper.

Remove the tops of the tomatoes by cutting around the edges to make lids. Spoon out the flesh and seeds and place in a bowl. Set aside with the lids.

Cut the zucchini in half crossways, then, at each end, chop off a 1 cm thick round to use as lids. To make the bases, using a knife and a spoon and leaving a 2 mm border around the edge, scoop the flesh out of each zucchini to make a deep cavity. Place the flesh in a small bowl.

Cut the top off the eggplant and reserve to use as a lid. Scoop out the flesh, leaving a 2 cm boarder around the edge. (This can be difficult, so take some time with it.) Add the flesh to the zucchini flesh.

Cut the tops off the capsicums and reserve as lids. Scoop out the membrane and seeds and discard.

Place the reserved zucchini and eggplant flesh in a food processor and process until finely chopped.

Heat the olive oil in a saucepan over medium heat, add the onion, garlic, chilli, parsley and mint and cook until the onion is softened, about 3 minutes. Stir in the chopped vegetable flesh and cook for 5–7 minutes. Add the reserved tomato flesh, the passata and tomato paste, sprinkle with salt and pepper and cook for 15 minutes. Pour in 250 ml (1 cup) of water, stir and simmer for 15–20 minutes. Stir in the quinoa and cook for 2 minutes. Remove from the heat. At this point, the quinoa will not be cooked – it will finish cooking in the oven.

Place all the vegetable bases in the prepared dish. Fill each one with the quinoa mixture, place a reserved lid on top and secure with a toothpick. Pour 125 ml (½ cup) of water into the dish, cover with foil and bake in the oven for 30 minutes. Remove the foil and continue to bake for 15–20 minutes until the quinoa is cooked.

Serve with a salad or some more yummy veggies.

SWEET POTATO *and* BASIL GNOCCHI WITH PESTO

SERVES: 6
PREP TIME: 30 MINUTES
COOK TIME: 25 MINUTES

750 g sweet potato, chopped
    into small chunks
500 g desiree potatoes,
    chopped into small chunks
1 teaspoon each of salt
    flakes and freshly ground
    black pepper
25 g (¼ cup) grated parmesan
2 teaspoons finely chopped
    basil leaves
300 g (2 cups) plain flour,
    sifted, plus extra for dusting
1 egg yolk
125 g (½ cup) Basil Pesto
    (page 113)

Cook the sweet potato and potato in a saucepan of salted boiling water for 20 minutes, or until tender. Drain well, transfer to a bowl and mash. Season with the salt and pepper, mix in the parmesan and basil and set aside to cool.

Add the flour to the sweet potato mixture and make a well in the centre. Add the egg yolk and stir to form a firm dough. (If the dough is too runny, mix in a little more flour.) Transfer to a lightly floured work surface and knead, dusting with more flour if the dough is sticky, until smooth and firm, about 5 minutes.

Cut the dough into eight equal portions. Roll each portion into a log, 2–3 cm in diameter. Using a lightly floured knife, cut each log into rounds about 2 cm in length and roll each of these rounds into small balls. Roll the prongs of a fork over each ball to make small grooves.

Cook the gnocchi in boiling salted water for 30 seconds, or until they rise to the surface. Scoop out with a slotted spoon and place in a large bowl. (You may need to cook your gnocchi in two batches.) Add the pesto, mix well, then divide between bowls and serve.

VEGGIE RISOTTO

SERVES: 6
PREP TIME: 20 MINUTES
COOK TIME: 30 MINUTES

1.5 litres (6 cups)
   vegetable stock
2 tablespoons olive oil
1 onion, diced
1 tablespoon finely chopped
   flat-leaf parsley, plus extra
   to serve
2 garlic cloves, crushed
¼ teaspoon chilli flakes
5 button mushrooms, cleaned
   and quartered
155 g butternut
   pumpkin, peeled and
   deseeded, chopped into
   bite-sized pieces
1 zucchini, cut into rounds
150 g (1 cup) cherry tomatoes
60 g (1 cup) broccoli florets
440 g (2 cups) arborio rice
125 ml (½ cup) white wine
   (such as pinot grigio or
   sauvignon blanc)
100 g (1 cup) grated parmesan,
   plus extra to serve
salt flakes and freshly ground
   black pepper

Pour the stock into a saucepan, place over low heat and bring to a simmer. Leave the stock simmering on low.

Heat the olive oil in a large saucepan over medium–high heat, add the onion, parsley, garlic and chilli flakes and cook, stirring occasionally, for 3 minutes, or until the onion is softened. Add the mushrooms, pumpkin, zucchini, cherry tomatoes and broccoli and cook, stirring, for 5 minutes. Remove from the pan and set aside.

Add the rice, white wine and 250 ml (1 cup) of simmering stock to the pan, reduce the heat to medium and give everything a good stir. Continue to stir until the liquid is absorbed, then add another cup of stock. Repeat this process. When you have added 3 cups of stock, return the vegetable mixture to the pan.

Continue stirring and adding the stock, ensuring each cup is absorbed before pouring in the next. Once you have added all the stock, test the rice. It should be tender and the mixture creamy. If not, add a cup of boiling water to the risotto and continue to cook for another 5 minutes or so. Remove from the heat and add the parmesan, and some salt and pepper. Stir and taste. Add more seasoning to your liking and serve with a sprinkle of extra parsley and some more parmesan.

 *You must use warm vegetable stock while cooking risotto.*

BLACK BEAN LETTUCE CUPS

SERVES: 4
PREP TIME: 10 MINUTES
COOK TIME: 25 MINUTES

1 tablespoon olive oil

1 onion, diced

3 garlic cloves, crushed

1 small red chilli, finely chopped

1 teaspoon ground cumin

125 ml (½ cup) vegetable stock

2 tomatoes, diced

1 tablespoon tomato paste

salt flakes and freshly ground
    black pepper

1 × 400 g can black
    beans, drained

2 tablespoons finely chopped
    coriander leaves, plus extra
    to serve

8 iceberg lettuce leaves

½ small avocado, finely sliced

Heat the olive oil in a frying pan over medium heat, add the onion, garlic and chilli and cook for 5 minutes, or until the onion is softened. Stir in the cumin, vegetable stock, tomato and tomato paste and cook for 10 minutes, or until simmering and fragrant. Season with salt and pepper.

Add the beans to the tomato mixture and cook for a further 5–10 minutes, until reduced and thick (you don't want this to be runny). Stir through the coriander.

Spoon the bean mixture into the lettuce cups and serve with the avocado and a sprinkle of coriander.

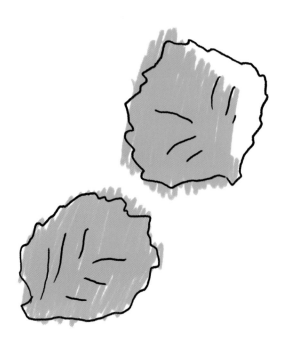

SWEET POTATO NACHOS

SERVES: 3
PREP TIME: 15 MINUTES
COOK TIME: 50 MINUTES

2 sweet potatoes, cut into
    4 mm thick rounds
salt flakes and freshly ground
    black pepper
olive oil, for drizzling and frying
½ onion, diced
1 garlic clove, crushed
1 teaspoon chilli flakes
1 teaspoon smoked paprika
1 × 400 g can black
    beans, drained
1 ripe avocado, diced
¼ red onion, grated
juice of ½ lemon
75 g (½ cup) grated mozzarella
2 tomatoes, diced

Preheat the oven to 200°C. Line a large baking tray with baking paper.

Arrange the sweet potato in a single layer on the lined tray. Sprinkle on some salt and pepper and drizzle with olive oil. Roast in the oven for 35 minutes, or until crisp on the edges.

Heat a splash of olive oil in a small saucepan over medium–high heat, add the diced onion, garlic, chilli flakes and paprika and cook for 5 minutes, or until the onion is softened. Stir in the black beans and cook for a further 5 minutes.

Place the avocado in a bowl and mash with the grated onion and lemon juice until smooth.

Arrange a layer of sweet potato chips in a baking dish. Add the beans and scatter over the cheese. Bake in the oven for 5 minutes, or until the cheese is melted. Top with the avocado and tomato and eat straightaway.

~3 WAYS~
PIZZA BASE

MOROCCAN QUINOA CRUST

VEGAN

MAKES: 2
PREP TIME: 5 MINUTES
COOK TIME: 55 MINUTES

1 tablespoon olive oil, plus extra
   for drizzling
100 g (½ cup) quinoa, rinsed
45 g (1 cup) baby spinach leaves
½ teaspoon salt flakes
1 teaspoon Moroccan seasoning
salt flakes and freshly ground black pepper

Preheat the oven to 200°C. Line a pizza or baking tray with baking paper and drizzle with olive oil.

Cook the quinoa according to the packet instructions. Set aside to cool.

Place the quinoa in a food processor and add 1 tablespoon of water, the spinach, salt, Moroccan seasoning and olive oil. Blitz until the mixture is smooth and spreadable. Add more water if needed, and have a little taste. Season accordingly.

Divide the mixture in half and place in two mounds on the prepared tray. Shape into two discs about 10 cm in diameter and 1 cm thick. Bake in the oven for 15 minutes, then, using a spatula, carefully lift and flip the crust. Return to the oven to bake for a further 15 minutes, or until lightly browned.

Add your fave toppings and pop back in the oven for 5–10 minutes.

Some yummy pizza toppings that work well with cauliflower crust include olives, mushrooms, red capsicum, rocket, red onion, feta and pineapple.

The Moroccan quinoa crust is my favourite of these pizza bases. This goes best with some ham, tomato, red onion, feta and fresh basil scattered over the top.

Broccoli pizza crust is AMAZING with veggies. Try topping yours with mushrooms, red capsicum, roasted pumpkin, onion and rocket.

CAULIFLOWER CRUST

VEGETARIAN · GLUTEN-FREE

MAKES: 2
PREP TIME: 5 MINUTES
COOK TIME: 50 MINUTES

olive oil, for drizzling
1 head of cauliflower, roughly chopped
2 eggs
35 g (⅓ cup) grated parmesan
¼ teaspoon chilli flakes
½ teaspoon dried oregano
salt flakes and freshly ground black pepper

Preheat the oven to 200°C. Grease a pizza or baking tray with olive oil.

Place the cauliflower in a food processor and whiz until finely chopped. (You want the cauliflower to resemble rice grains.)

Transfer the cauliflower to a steamer basket and place over a saucepan of simmering water. Cover with the lid and steam for 8–10 minutes, until tender. Another option is to steam the cauliflower in the microwave on high for 5–7 minutes. Leave to cool.

Add the eggs, parmesan, chilli flakes, dried oregano and salt and pepper to the cauliflower and mix to combine.

Divide the mixture in half and place on the prepared tray in two mounds. Evenly spread out to form two discs about 10 cm in diameter and 1 cm thick. Drizzle on a little olive oil and bake in the oven for 15 minutes. Using a spatula, carefully turn over the crusts (they're quite tender at this stage) and bake for a further 15 minutes, or until lightly browned and firm.

Add your fave toppings and return to the oven for another 5–10 minutes.

BROCCOLI CRUST

VEGETARIAN · GLUTEN-FREE

MAKES: 2
PREP TIME: 5 MINUTES
COOK TIME: 50 MINUTES

olive oil, for drizzling
2 heads of broccoli, roughly chopped
2 eggs
35 g (⅓ cup) grated parmesan
¼ teaspoon chilli flakes
½ teaspoon dried oregano
salt flakes and freshly ground black pepper

Preheat the oven to 200°C. Grease a pizza or baking tray with olive oil.

Place the broccoli in a food processor and process until finely chopped (don't make it a paste, leave some rough texture).

Transfer the broccoli to a steamer basket and place over a saucepan of simmering water. Cover with the lid and steam for 8–10 minutes, until tender. Another option is to steam the broccoli in the microwave on high for 8–10 minutes. Leave to cool.

If the broccoli looks super watery, place in a clean Chux cloth and squeeze out as much liquid as possible.

Place the broccoli in a large bowl and add the eggs, parmesan, chilli flakes, dried oregano and salt and pepper and mix to combine.

Divide the broccoli mixture in half. Place on the prepared tray in two mounds and spread out to form two discs about 10 cm in diameter and 1 cm thick. Drizzle on some olive oil and bake in the oven for 15 minutes. Flip over carefully using a spatula and bake for a further 15 minutes, or until lightly browned and firm.

Add your fave toppings and pop back in the oven for 5–10 minutes.

EASY PEASY VEGGIE LAKSA

SERVES: 3–4
PREP TIME: 15 MINUTES
COOK TIME: 15 MINUTES

2 tablespoons peanut oil, plus
   extra if needed
250 ml (1 cup) vegetable stock
600 ml canned coconut milk
1 head of broccoli,
   cut into florets
2 carrots, finely sliced
3 bok choy, cut into bite-sized
   pieces (optional)
6 button mushrooms, cleaned
   and halved
10 baby corn cobs, cut into
   bite-sized pieces
250 g hokkien noodles
1 small handful of
   coriander leaves
1 handful of bean sprouts

DIY LAKSA PASTE
6 mild long red
   chillies, deseeded
2 teaspoons shrimp paste
2 onions, quartered
2 tablespoons finely
   grated galangal
2 lemongrass stalks, white part
   only, roughly chopped
1 teaspoon ground turmeric
1 tablespoon cumin seeds
3 garlic cloves
1 teaspoon ground coriander
2 tablespoons lime juice
2 tablespoons fish sauce

Place all the paste ingredients in a food processor and whiz until completely smooth. If needed, add a touch of peanut oil to blend.

Heat the peanut oil in a wok or large saucepan over high heat, add half the laksa paste and fry for 2 minutes, or until fragrant. Pour in the vegetable stock and coconut milk and cook, stirring occasionally, for 5 minutes. Add the broccoli, carrot, bok choy (if using), mushrooms and corn and cook for 5 minutes, or until the veggies are cooked to your liking.

Meanwhile, cook the noodles according to the packet instructions. Drain and divide between serving bowls. Using a ladle, spoon the laksa and lots of veggies into each bowl. Top with the coriander and bean sprouts and eat straightaway.

→ *The remaining laksa paste will last, stored in an airtight container in the fridge for up to 2 weeks. It's a great marinade for fish!*

HOKKIEN NOODLE STIR-FRY

SERVES: 4
PREP TIME: 15 MINUTES
COOK TIME: 20 MINUTES

2 tablespoons sesame oil

2 tablespoons soy sauce

2 tablespoons oyster sauce

½ teaspoon chilli flakes,
    plus extra to serve

½ onion, diced

1 garlic clove, crushed

1 cm piece of ginger, grated

1 bok choy, finely sliced

1 head of broccoli, cut
    into florets

2 carrots, finely sliced

8 baby corn cobs, chopped
    into bite-sized pieces

½ red capsicum, finely sliced

5 button mushrooms, cleaned
    and quartered

¼ red cabbage, shredded

250 g hokkien noodles

2 tablespoons coriander leaves

To make the dressing, in a small bowl, mix 1 tablespoon of the sesame oil with the soy sauce, oyster sauce and chilli flakes. Set aside.

Heat the remaining sesame oil in a wok or large saucepan over high heat, add the onion, garlic and ginger and cook for 2 minutes, or until the onion is softened. Throw in all the veggies and stir-fry for 10–15 minutes, until tender.

Cook the noodles according to the packet instructions, drain and add to the veggies. Toss through the dressing and cook for 2 minutes to allow the noodles to soak up the flavour.

Divide the stir-fry between serving bowls, scatter over the coriander and more chilli flakes if you like it spicy.

VEGETARIAN · DAIRY-FREE

THAI FRIED RICE

SERVES: 4
PREP TIME: 10 MINUTES
COOK TIME: 15 MINUTES

2 tablespoons olive oil

3 spring onions, finely sliced

2 garlic cloves, crushed

100 g green beans, topped
   and tailed

30 g (½ cup) broccoli
   florets, chopped

1 small red capsicum,
   finely sliced

5 button mushrooms,
   cleaned and halved

1 handful of roughly chopped
   Thai basil leaves, plus extra
   whole leaves to serve

370 g (2 cups) cooked
   jasmine rice

3 tablespoons soy sauce

salt flakes and freshly ground
   black pepper

1 small red chilli, finely
   sliced (optional)

Heat the olive oil in a wok or large saucepan over high heat. Add the spring onion and garlic and cook, stirring, for 2 minutes, or until fragrant. Add all the vegetables and the chopped Thai basil and stir-fry for 5 minutes, or until cooked to your liking.

Stir the cooked rice into the vegetables, then drizzle on the soy sauce and stir. Sprinkle with salt and pepper and stir again.

Serve the fried rice with the extra Thai basil scattered over the top and sprinkle on the chilli if you like it spicy.

GARLIC FOCACCIA *with* HUMMUS *and* ROASTED TOMATOES

SERVES: 2
PREP TIME: 15 MINUTES
COOK TIME: 25 MINUTES

2 tomatoes, halved
½ teaspoon dried oregano
2½ tablespoons olive oil
2 garlic cloves, crushed
1 focaccia, halved
pinch of chilli flakes (optional)

DIY HUMMUS
(MAKES 330 G [1½ CUPS])
2 × 400 g cans
   chickpeas, drained
2 tablespoons lemon juice
1 garlic clove, crushed
125 ml (½ cup) olive oil,
   plus extra if needed
2 tablespoons hulled tahini
sprinkle of salt flakes and
   freshly ground black pepper
2 tablespoons roughly
   chopped coriander

Preheat the oven to 180°C. Line a baking tray with baking paper.

To make the hummus, combine the chickpeas, lemon juice, garlic, olive oil, tahini and salt and pepper in a food processor and whiz. Throw in the coriander and blitz until smooth. Set aside until you're ready to plate up.

Place the tomatoes on the lined tray and sprinkle with salt, pepper and the dried oregano. Drizzle over a little of the olive oil, then bake in the oven for 20 minutes, or until the tomato halves are softened and collapsed. Place under the grill for 5 minutes to get that gorgeous brown colour.

Combine the garlic and remaining olive oil in a small bowl. Brush over the focaccia and place under the grill for 5 minutes, or until lightly browned.

Smear the hummus on the toasted focaccia, add two roasted tomato halves and sprinkle on the chilli flakes if you like some heat. Enjoy!

Hummus is great because it's super versatile. Use as a dressing for roast veggies, as a dip or spread on toast or wraps. Keep any leftover hummus in an airtight container in the fridge for up to 2 weeks.

BAKED FALAFEL

MAKES: 8
PREP TIME: 10 MINUTES,
PLUS OVERNIGHT SOAKING
COOK TIME: 25 MINUTES

220 g (1 cup) dried chickpeas
1 onion, quartered
1 garlic clove, crushed
1 handful of flat-leaf
   parsley leaves
1 handful of coriander leaves
½ teaspoon baking powder
½ teaspoon ground cumin
½ teaspoon salt flakes
¼ teaspoon freshly ground
   black pepper
1 teaspoon lemon juice

Place the chickpeas in a large bowl and cover with plenty of water. Cover and set aside to soak overnight.

The next day, preheat the oven to 200°C. Line a baking tray with baking paper.

Drain the chickpeas and rinse well. Place in a food processor and add the onion, garlic, parsley, coriander, baking powder, cumin, salt, pepper and lemon juice. Whiz until completely mixed but don't let the mixture turn into a runny paste.

Divide the falafel mixture into eight equal portions. Shape into patties and place on the lined tray. Bake in the oven for 25 minutes, turning over halfway, until lightly browned.

You MUST make your falafels with dried chickpeas – don't try to use canned as they will not work.

SWEET POTATO SAUSAGE ROLLS

MAKES: 24
PREP TIME: 15 MINUTES
COOK TIME: 1 HOUR,
10 MINUTES

1 kg sweet potato, chopped into
   rough chunks

¼ teaspoon ground turmeric

¼ teaspoon smoked paprika,
   plus extra for sprinkling

pinch of ground cumin

pinch of salt flakes and freshly
   ground black pepper

2 tablespoons olive oil

1 onion, finely diced

200 g feta

60 g (½ cup) walnuts, crushed

2 tablespoons finely
   chopped coriander

1 egg

2 tablespoons sesame seeds

6 frozen puff pastry
   sheets, thawed

tomato ketchup or sweet chilli
   sauce, to serve

Preheat the oven to 180°C. Line a baking tray with baking paper.

Place the sweet potato in a bowl, sprinkle on the turmeric, paprika, cumin and salt and pepper. Drizzle on 1 tablespoon of the olive oil and toss to mix thoroughly. Transfer to the lined tray and roast in the oven for 40 minutes, or until the sweet potato is tender.

Heat the remaining olive oil in a frying pan over medium heat, add the onion and cook for 5 minutes, or until translucent. Remove from the heat.

Tip the sweet potato into a bowl, add the feta, cooked onion, walnuts and coriander and mix well.

Whisk the egg in a small bowl, and have your sesame seeds and paprika handy.

Take one pastry sheet and, about 2 cm from one edge, spoon on one-sixth of the sweet potato mixture in a log shape. Roll up as tightly as possible and transfer, seam down, to the lined tray. Repeat with the remaining pastry sheets and sweet potato mixture.

Cut each sweet potato roll into four pieces (or as many as you like) and brush with the whisked egg. Sprinkle generously with the sesame seeds and extra paprika. Bake in the oven for 30 minutes, or until golden brown. Serve hot with some tomato ketchup or sweet chilli sauce.

 Don't steam the sweet potato – it gives the sausage rolls a very different taste.

SWEET POTATO
and LENTIL PATTIES

MAKES: 6
PREP TIME: 15 MINUTES
COOK TIME: 1 HOUR

1 sweet potato, chopped into
    small chunks
salt flakes and freshly ground
    black pepper
olive oil, for drizzling
100 g (½ cup) dried red
    lentils, cooked
1 tablespoon lemon juice
1 teaspoon smoked paprika
1 teaspoon ground cumin
pinch of cayenne pepper
3 tablespoons plain flour
1 small handful of coriander
    leaves, finely chopped, plus
    extra to serve

Preheat the oven to 180°C. Line a baking tray with baking paper.

Place the sweet potato on the lined tray, sprinkle with salt and pepper and drizzle on a little olive oil. Roast in the oven for 30 minutes, or until the sweet potato is tender. Set aside to cool.

Transfer the sweet potato to a bowl and mash. Add the lentils, lemon juice, paprika, cumin, cayenne pepper, flour and coriander, sprinkle with salt and pepper and mix thoroughly. Shape into six patties.

Drizzle a little olive oil over the lined tray, then add the patties. Bake in the oven for 15 minutes, flip over and bake for a further 15 minutes, or until lightly browned.

Scatter coriander leaves over your sweet potato and lentil patties and serve with burger buns and yummy veggies or with any salad.

To cook lentils, pour 375 ml (1½ cups) of water into a saucepan and add 100 g (½ cup) dried red lentils. Bring to the boil, cover tightly with a lid, then reduce the heat to low and simmer for 15 minutes, or until the lentils are tender.

VEGETARIAN PIZZA

SERVES: 1
PREP TIME: 10 MINUTES
COOK TIME: 15 MINUTES

1 pita bread
olive oil, for brushing
2 tablespoons Basil Pesto
  (page 113)
½ tomato, finely sliced
½ avocado, sliced
2 button mushrooms, cleaned
  and finely sliced
2 marinated artichoke hearts,
  drained and quartered
5 pitted kalamata olives
2 basil leaves
45 g feta

Preheat the oven to 180°C.

Brush one side of the pita bread with olive oil.

Place the pita bread, oiled side down, on a baking tray and spread on an even layer of pesto. Add the tomato, avocado, mushrooms, artichokes and olives, scatter over the basil and crumble on the feta. Bake in the oven for 10–15 minutes, until cooked to your liking.

INDEX

ACKNOWLEDGEMENTS

Anna Itsines: Thank you SO much to my beautiful mother who helped test, taste and alter the recipes! This book wouldn't have been done without all your amazing help.

Mitch Caon: Thank you to my beautiful partner who assisted in all aspects of this book, co-writing and co–taste testing! I appreciate all the love and support you gave me through this entire process.

Lyndi Cohen: This book was reviewed by dietitian and nutritionist Lyndi Cohen. Lyndi Cohen is an Accredited Practising Dietitian known as The Nude Nutritionist for her stripped bare, back-to-basics approach to nutrition. Lyndi experienced an incredible health transformation and lost over 20 kg when she quit dieting and stopped emotional eating. She's now one of Australia's most well known dietitians, appears on national TV several times a week and runs the hugely popular blog www.lyndicohen.com.

Thank you to Pan Macmillan, especially my publisher Ingrid Ohlsson, creative manager Megan Pigott and editors Danielle Walker and Megan Johnston. Thank you to the amazing shoot team – Jeremy Simons, Vanessa Austin and Dixie Elliott – and my designer Alissa Dinallo for all your hard work.

First published 2018 in Macmillan
by Pan Macmillan Australia Pty Limited
1 Market Street, Sydney, New South Wales
Australia 2000

A CIP catalogue record for this book is available from the National Library of
Australia: http://catalogue.nla.gov.au

Design by Alissa Dinallo
Photography by Jeremy Simons with additional photography on
pages 46–55 by Rob Palmer
Prop and food styling by Vanessa Austin
Food preparation by Dixie Elliott and Tammi Kwok
Editing by Danielle Walker
Recipe editing by Megan Johnston
Typesetting by Post Pre-press Group, Brisbane
Index by Frances Paterson
Make-up by Leah Baines
Colour + reproduction by Splitting Image Colour Studio
Printed and bound in China by Imago Printing International Limited

10 9 8 7 6 5 4 3 2 1